Swords of the Viking Age

Nomenclature of Viking Age Swords

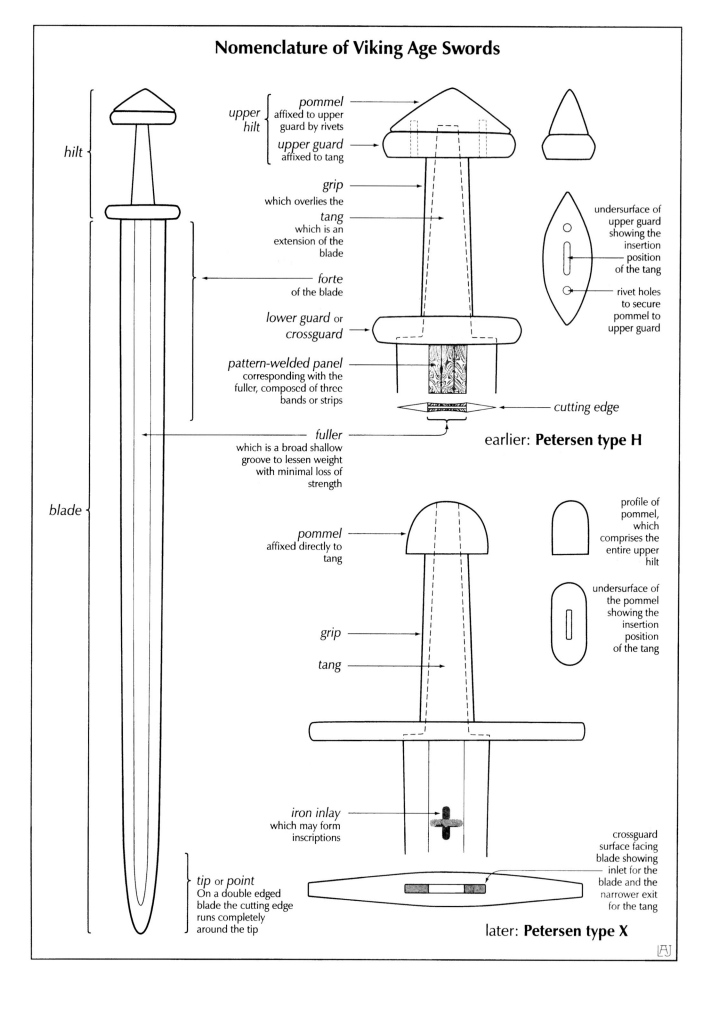

hilt

upper hilt {

pommel
affixed to upper guard by rivets

upper guard
affixed to tang

grip
which overlies the

tang
which is an extension of the blade

forte
of the blade

lower guard or *crossguard*

pattern-welded panel
corresponding with the fuller, composed of three bands or strips

cutting edge

fuller
which is a broad shallow groove to lessen weight with minimal loss of strength

undersurface of upper guard showing the insertion position of the tang

rivet holes to secure pommel to upper guard

earlier: **Petersen type H**

blade

pommel
affixed directly to tang

grip

tang

profile of pommel, which comprises the entire upper hilt

undersurface of the pommel showing the insertion position of the tang

iron inlay
which may form inscriptions

crossguard surface facing blade showing inlet for the blade and the narrower exit for the tang

tip or *point*
On a double edged blade the cutting edge runs completely around the tip

later: **Petersen type X**

AJ

Swords of the Viking Age

INTRODUCED BY

Ewart Oakeshott

CATALOGUE OF EXAMPLES COMPILED AND DESCRIBED BY

Ian G. Peirce

The Boydell Press

First published 2002
The Boydell Press, Woodbridge
Reprinted in hardback and paperback 2004
Reprinted in paperback 2005

ISBN 0 85115 914 1 hardback
ISBN 1 84383 089 2 paperback

The Boydell Press is an imprint of Boydell & Brewer Ltd
PO Box 9, Woodbridge, Suffolk IP12 3DF, UK
and of Boydell & Brewer Inc.
PO Box 41026, Rochester, NY 14604-4126, USA
website: www.boydellandbrewer.com

A catalogue record for this book is available from the British Library

The Library of Congress has cataloged the hardcover edition as follows:

Peirce, Ian G., 1941-
    Swords of the Viking age / text by Ian G. Peirce ; introduced by Ewart Oakeshott.
        p. cm.
    ISBN 0-85115-914-1 (alk. paper)
    l. Swords, Medieval--Scandinavia. 2. Vikings--Material culture. I. Title.
U854 .P45 2002
623.4'41--dc21

                                                                                    2002028186

Designed, illustrated and captioned by Lee A. Jones

Printed in Great Britain by Short Run Press Ltd

Supplementary material may be found at www.vikingsword.com/vbook

Table of Contents

Preface & Acknowledgements   vii
Ian G. Peirce

Introduction to the Viking Sword   1
Ewart Oakeshott

Overview of Hilt and Blade Classifications   15
Lee A. Jones

Colour Plates I–VIII   following 24

Catalogue of Examples   25
Ian G. Peirce

Blade Construction and Pattern-Welding   145
Lee A. Jones

Index   152

Bergens Museum Oldsaksamling, Bergen, Norway
B883   Norway, Jarlsberg og Larvik (Vestfold), Larvik, Hedrum
           (Lorange pl. VI), I
B2605   Norway, Søndre Bergenhus, Opheim, paa Vossestranden
           (Lorange pl. V), II
B2799   Norway, Søndre Bergenhus (Hordaland), Ulvik, Torblaa
           (Petersen pl. III), 114
B6748a   Norway, Nordre Bergenhus (Sogn og Fjordane), Forde,
           Hjelle (Petersen pl. I), 46

British Museum, London, England
1848, 10-21 1   England, Lincoln, River Witham opposite Monks
                 Abbey, 77–79
1856, 7-1 1404   England, London, River Thames in King's Reach, off
                 the Temple, 80–81
1864, 1-27 3   Ireland, Co. Limerick, near Holycross, Lough Gur,
                 near Grange, 95
1873, 12-19 233 Norway, Oslo, Aker, Hoff, Hov, burial mound, 38
1887, 2-9 1   England, London, River Thames at Temple Church,
                 104–105
1891, 9-5 3   England, Kew, River Thames, 90–91
1912, 7-23 1   England, Durham, near Hurbuck, 76
1915, 5-4 1   England, Middlesex, Edmonton, River Lea, 110–111

Chertsey Museum, Chertsey, England
CHYMS 2465 England, Chertsey, Mixnam's Pit, 98–99

Musée de l'Armée, Paris, France
J1   70–71
J3   84–86
J4   142–144
JPO 2241   131
JPO 2242   128–130
JPO 2249   52–53
JPO 2251   120–121
JPO 2253   118–119
JPO 2262   74–75

National Museum of Ireland, Dublin, Ireland
1928:382   Ireland, Ballinderry bog, drainage ditch, 63–65
1936:3763 Ireland, County Kildare, Wheelam, 82–83
1988:226   Ireland, County Tipperary, Lough Derg (New Curraghmore),
           140–141
E122:94   Ireland, Dublin, Christ Church Place, 109
WK-5   Ireland, Kilmainham, 66–67
WK-21   Ireland, Island-Bridge and Kilmainham cemetery, 58–59
WK-24   Ireland, County West Meath, Parish of Rathconrath,
           Dungolman River, 56–57
WK-25   Ireland, County Limerick, near Askeaton, 28–29
WK-31   Ireland, Dublin, Kilmainham, 39
WK-33   Ireland, Kilmainham, 42–43

Nationalmuseet, Copenhagen, Denmark
780-4   100–101
C1572   Denmark, N. Jutland, Søndersø, Bjørnsholm, 44–45
C3118   Denmark, Bildsø, 30–31
C5818   Denmark, København, Volborg, Osted, 112–113
C6374   150
C8727   Denmark, Holbæk, Ars, Tissø, 115
C16430   Denmark, lake near Søborg Castle, 106–107
C24550   Denmark, København, Smørum, Måløv, Sørup, 50–51
C24554   Denmark, Tude River, between Heinng and Naesby, 48–49
C25340   Denmark, Nydam, 146

Suomen kansallismuse, Helsinki, Finland
NM 704   Finland, Jämsä, 136–137
NM 1174:1 Finland, Satakunta, Kokemäki, Leikkimäki, 138–139
NM 2022:1 Finland, Huolila, Lahdinko, Vehmaa, 148–149
NM 2033:1 Finland, Padasjoki, 122–123
NM 2767   Finland, Rapola, Valkeakoski (formerly Sääksmäki), 8
NM 2886:11 Finland, Hukari, Sakoinen, Vesilahti, 127
NM 3631:1 Finland, Lappland, Rovaniemi, Marikkovaara, 134–135
NM 6245A:1 Finland, Jussila, Tiihala, Kangasala, 60–62
NM 11840   Finland, Vammala (formerly Tryvää), railway station, 132–
           133
NM 18402:1 Finland, Häme, Hämeenlinna, Peltorinne, 54–55

Trondheim Museum Oldsaksamling, Trondheim, Norway
T3107   Norway, Søndre Trondhjem (Sør-Trondelag), Aafjorden,
           Bredvold (Petersen fig. 123), 114

Universitetets Oldsaksamling, Oslo, Norway
C237   Norway, Oppland, Vaage, Sandbu farm, 102–103
C257   Norway, Hedemarken, 96–97
C777   Norway, Buskerud, Hallingdalen, Naesby, Flaa Sogn parish,
           Vig farm, 36–37
C1554   Norway, Kristians (Oppland), Ø Slidre, Dale (Petersen
           fig. 71), 47
C1779   Norway, Nordre Bergenhus (Sogn og Fjordane), Aardal,
           Seim (Petersen fig. 122), 110
C3210   Norway, Hedemark, Korsgården Ånses., 108
C3211   Norway, Hedemark, Korsgården Ånses., 108
C4115   Norway, Akershus, Fet, Nordby (Petersen fig. 103), 86
C4397   Norway, Buskerud, Lier, Svere Farm, 92–93
C6409   Norway, Akershus, Eidsvold, Habberstad (Petersen
           fig. 67), 47
C11014   Norway, Hedemark, Åmot, Kilde farm, 72–73
C12009   Norway, Jarlsberg og Larvik (Vestfold), Hedrum, Rimstad
           (Petersen fig. 72), 46
C13848a   Norway, Akershus, Løiten parish, Vestre Berg, 87–89
C16001   Norway, Kristians (Oppland), V. Slidre, Jarstad (Petersen
           fig. 53), 35
C16380   Norway, Smaalene (Østfold), Rygge, Gunnarsby (Petersen
           fig. 105), 88
C18454   Norway, Lesjeskogen, Mølmen, Skoven, 108, VIII
C18798   Norway, Nedenes (Aust-Agder), Valle Sogn, Rygnestad farm,
           126
C19763   Norway, Kristians (Oppland), Jevnaker, Lunner parish,
           Kjørven farm, 94
C20317   Norway, Nordland, Hol Lødingen parish, Steinvik farm,
           32–33, IV
C23127   Norway, Oppland, N. Aurdal, Nes, Strandefjorden, VII
C24217   Norway, Telemark, Hjartdal parish, North Arhus farm, 40–41
C24244   Norway, Telemark, Rauland, Mogen, 86
C25576b   Norway, Buskerud, Sigdal parish, Ostby farm, 68–69
C26494   Norway, Oppland, Valdres, Østre Slidre, Rogne parish,
           Skatteby farm, 116–117

Private Collections
-          9
-          26–27
-          Holland, Province Limburg, Maas river between Horn and
           Roermond, 34–35
-          Norway, Oppland, Ringebu, 86
-          Spain, 124–125
-          Holland, Province Noord-Brabant, Kessel, Maas River, V
-          Sweden, VI
-          VI

Preface & Acknowledgements
Ian G. Peirce

Selecting, inspecting and writing the various drafts of the swords contained in this book has been a source of great joy.

Initially, the swords selected were to be whole, complete weapons, but it swiftly became evident that many of the incomplete, fragmented swords could not be ignored. The swords are classified initially by Petersen's hilt types, followed by Oakeshott's blade types.

The precise dating of swords is not always easy. However, a combination of the data presented by Jan Petersen, with Geibig's analysis of blade types and the typology and dating of Jakobsson, produced an acceptable and valuable equation.

The subjective term *wieldability* has been included in order to give some indication of how the weapon performed in the hand and of course is much dependent upon the position of the centre of gravity and the arm and shoulder strength of the man.

Lee Jones had the inspiration to see the need for a book on Viking Age swords, and indeed commissioned and funded the whole project. This resulted in he and I visiting the major museums in Scandinavia, both in 1993 and 1994 and I went again in 1998. I also had the opportunity to visit both the National Museum of Ireland, Dublin and the Musée de l'Armée, Paris on several occasions.

To Lee, I shall be eternally grateful for the opportunities and challenges the project presented.

There are two others to whom I am greatly in debt: Else Roesdahl and Maylis Baylé. Else, who I met at the Battle Conference, put me in touch with the key people at the museums in Scandinavia, and without her help, access to those fabulous collections may have proved difficult, especially in the area of actually handling the weapons and inspecting them closely.

Maylis has been a friend and fellow member of the Battle Conference for close on a quarter of a century, and her letters of introduction enabled me to gain access to the splendid collection in the Musée de l'Armée.

Thanks are also due to my former colleagues Dave Smith and Mary Robertson of St. Richard's School, Bexhill-on-Sea and Alina Plass, all who helped with numerous translations.

The hospitality and generosity of the museum staff was overwhelming.

My grateful thanks to Helga Schütze, Lars Jørgensen, Niels-Knud Liebgott, and especially, Anne Pedersen, for unstinting help, all of the National Museum of Denmark.

I am indebted to Jean-Paul Sage-Freney and Anne Pavard, both of the Musée de l'Armée and Raghnall Ó Floinn, Andy Halpin and Paul Mullarky of the National Museum of Ireland. All contributed much to the quality of my research.

At the Universitetets Oldsaksamling, Oslo, the following are remembered for the generosity of their knowledge and time: Irmelin Martens, Heid Gjøstein Resi, Karin Knoph, Vigdis Hov, Ove Holst, Britt Myhrvold, Eirik Irgens Johnsten and Silje Opdahl.

The swords at the National Museum of Finland, Helsinki, were very special and I am extremely grateful to those of the National Board of Antiquities, namely, Leena Ruonavaara, J.P. Taavitsainen, Leena Söyrinki-Harmo and especially Leena Tomanterä, for their many kindnesses, both in 1994 and since.

The final collection to be viewed and written up was that in the British Museum and sincere thanks are due to Lesley Webster for allowing me to work on the swords at short notice and to Barry Ager and Sovati Smith.

I am indebted to Christian Segebade of the Bundesanstalt für Materialforschung und-prüfung, Berlin, for an excellent scientific report on the sword presented on pp. 26–27 and to David Oliver for his friendship, help and encouragement.

It is appropriate for me to thank my friend Ewart Oakeshott, who did much to fuel my enthusiasm for the study of medieval swords.

My wife Elizabeth has been a great source of encouragement during this lengthy project and I thank her not only for her administrative skills, but also for the manner in which she has patiently endured my sometimes feverish passion for the subject.

Finally, the production of this volume owes much to the dedication and efficiency of Dr. Richard Barber, Caroline Palmer and all the staff of Boydell & Brewer.

Cowbeech, East Sussex   Ian Peirce

Introduction to the Viking Sword
Ewart Oakeshott

'Who can separate a man and his sword? One is worth nothing without the other.'[1]

The sentiment behind this aphorism is the strong weft upon which the whole vivid fabric of Viking life and culture is woven. Though this is made manifest in every saga, every poem and kenning, the importance of the sword is given no place in the large body of scholarly publications concerning the Age of the Vikings written in the English language. Their efficiency as traders, businessmen and bankers, farmers and craftsmen is celebrated in careful detail. Of course their sea-raiding in search of plunder, and the sacking of monasteries could not be evaded, but even this is passed over rather hurriedly so as not to mar the picture of the pleasant and peaceable Viking. A striking example of this avoidance of the sword is shown in an illustration in a popular book. This is a very careful and clear watercolour drawing of grave goods taken out of a grave near Claughton in Lancashire, opened in the 1840's. There were many pieces of jewellery, beautifully drawn and carefully described in detail in 1847; but there is one item which is totally ignored, merely referred to as *other pieces of ironwork*. This other piece of ironwork is a fine sword of a most unusual form for the Age of the Vikings. If it were to have emerged on its own, without the associated grave goods, it would have been assigned to a period 1250–1350. It has a wide disc pommel and a long grip, some seven inches, though the cross–or the lower hilt–is of the usual Viking thick stubby type. The blade is too badly corroded to form an opinion upon it. But it is undoubtedly a Viking Age sword, totally ignored. Had this sword been appreciated and accepted as of Viking origin a century ago, all our thinking and classifying of medieval swords would have been different, and much more accurate. This drawing is now in the library of the Society of Antiquaries in London.

This avoidance of the sword's role in the lifestyle of the Vikings is all the more strange considering the wealth of vivid and evocative phrases–kennings–which abound in all the Norse literature and particularly the great body of poetry.

The most frequently used kenning is *Ancient Heirloom*. We find it everywhere, and it certainly meant just what it says, for these swords were nearly always handed on from generation to generation, and any one of them may have been in use for a couple of centuries. The kennings of course applied to any sword rather than to any one in particular; but each sword was deemed to be a personality in its own right, and it had its personal name. A great many of these names survive in the poems and sagas–even in wills. It is of such importance that though we have the swords, and the names, they can never coincide. But when the photographs here are looked at, it is well to remember that even though now they are archaeological artefacts, once they lived and were loved and named. Often a sword was given to a child at birth, and often a Viking with a little son would bring his own sword, when the boy was old enough to grasp the hilt and understand what his father told him. *This is my sword. Her name is Hilditonn. My father had her, and his father before. Now she is mine, and will soon be yours.* Then he would recount what feats the sword had achieved in the hands of the boy's Grandfather and Great-Grandfather, and, of course, his own. A sort of Curriculum Vitae. In this way the life-stories of swords were handed on.

Davidson puts the whole ethos of the sword most succinctly:[2]

> Thus the sword was closely associated with much of what was most significant in a man's life–family ties, loyalty to his lord, the duties of a king, the excitement of battle, the attainment of manhood, and the last funeral rites. It was something from which its owner was never never parted throughout his life, from the moment that he received it and had the right to wear it. He carried it in the king's hall and at law meetings, although on such occasions it was forbidden to draw it, and it might be fastened down in the scabbard. At night it hung above his bed, as we know from *Beowulf* and the Icelandic Sagas. A sudden attack often came at night, and to lose hold of one's sword, as King Æthelstan discovered, was a terrifying experience. If it had to be sent away to be resharpened, it was necessary to find another sword to take its place, and even this temporary substitution might cost a man dear. It was indeed, as is said in one of the Anglo–Saxon riddles, the prince's 'shoulder-companion', his close friend ever at his side, and 'the warrior's comrade'. Small wonder that Bersi the Dueller, famous swordsman and poet of the tenth century, declared that if he could no longer wield his sword, life held nothing more for him:
>
> > *The trolls may have my life indeed, when I can no more redden keen Laufi. Then you may carry the destroyer of the mailcoat's wand into the howe, without delay.*
>
> For a man who could no longer rely upon his sword had become a nonentity, a helpless figure relying on others for the protection of life, property, and reputation. The time had come to hand over the guardianship of the family, with the sword, to his descendants.

Many and varied were the types of sword hilt used by the Vikings; many also were the vivid and evocative poetic phrases which the skalds of the North used in their verses to replace the plain noun *sword*: 'Corpse-Bramble', 'War Snake', 'Viper', 'Hard-Edged Survivor of the Files', 'Battle-Flasher', 'Serpent of Blood', 'Leech of Wounds', 'Widow-Maker', 'The Shield's Bane', 'Odin's Flame', 'Ice of Battle', 'Dog of the Helmet', 'Torch of the Blood', 'The Sea-King's Fire', 'Harmer of War Knittings', 'Snake of the Byrnie' and perhaps the most frequently used one, particularly in Anglo-Saxon poems, 'Ancient Heirloom'. This, as a synonym for *sword*, may seem a little odd, but in fact it describes something very real. Moving from the period of the migrations into the Viking Age, we find that many of the swords used by characters in the Norse Sagas indeed were ancient heirlooms, swords either handed down in a family for generations, or taken out of burial-mounds for re-use, often a couple of centuries after their original interment. In the same way, many of the swords which were made new during the Viking Age (which we may call roughly between A.D. 750 and 1100) were still in active use as late as the 13th century. In the Swiss National Museum in Zurich, there is even a pattern-welded blade of 7th century date re-used with a 'katzbalger' hilt in the early 16th century.[3] There may be many other similar examples yet to be found. This period which we call the Viking Age was a linking time between the Heroic Age of the migrations and the Age of Chivalry; for the roving and raiding of the Vikings was the final manifestation of the migrations, while the Age of Chivalry began during the final century of Vikingdom, and was in fact the product of the Viking heroic ethos added to the imaginative romanticism of the Celtic peoples of France and Brittany and Western Britain.

So at the start of the Viking Age, swords from the Migration Period were still in use, and at its end we find that swords of types that have always been associated with the Age of Chivalry were put into the graves of Vikings.

In between these two 'periods' of swords, were the various types which are always known as 'Viking Swords'. A most complete and masterly study of these hilt-forms was published in Oslo, in 1919, by Dr. Jan Petersen.[4] His study was mostly confined to the hilts because the forms of blade did not vary much. Nothing to compare with Petersen's work has been done–nor, indeed, is it ever likely that more work will need to be done, so sound is his study. However, it is possible to reduce his 26 types and numerous sub-types to just nine, which makes the whole thing more manageable.

It is not important to know the place where any sword has been found in modern times, because all through the Middle ages, people were constantly on the move, none more so than warriors. To assert that, because an 11th century sword was found near a town in Southern England, it is probably English is nonsense. It would make as much sense to say that because the remains of a Junkers 88 aeroplane is found in a Norwegian fiord, it is probably Norwegian. These weapons got around with their owners. They were lost, captured in combat, given to a comrade, traded, or finally buried with a Viking who may have died on the shores of the Black Sea or in Africa, Spain, or Italy. However, having said that, we have to admit that where great numbers of the same kind of sword are found in the same region, then at least there is a little justification for stating that such a type did come from such and such a region. 'Came from' here means the type used in that place, not necessarily made there. Fashion was as potent a force in the Viking Age as it has been ever since, but there is little evidence as to where hilts–which showed the fashion–were made.

We can be fairly sure that blades, the best blades that is, were made in the Rhineland, where the town of Solingen later grew, and in the region of the old Roman Noricum (Southern Bavaria) where the Celts of the earlier Iron Age as well as the Romans obtained their swords, because in these two locations was found the finest iron.

Hilts of Types I and II can be assigned with some certainty to the Norwegians, who used these types and very probably made them. Over 330 examples of Type II have been found in Norway (most of them on one-edged swords, for which the Norwegians seem to have had a preference),

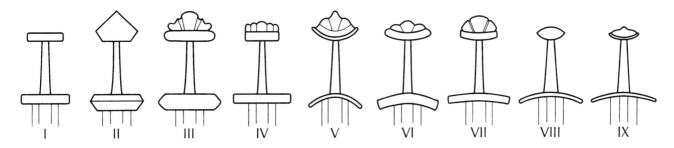

Fig. 1. I - VII. Wheeler's typology of Viking Age sword hilt types associated with British find-places, from R.E.M. Wheeler, *London and the Vikings* (London, 1927), fig. 13, p. 32. VIII - IX. Oakeshott's extension of the classification, from R. Ewart Oakeshott, *The Archaeology of Weapons* (London, 1960), fig. 57, p. 133. Drawing by Lee A. Jones.

some have been recorded from Sweden, and none at all from Denmark. In the British Isles, they occur along the line of the early Norwegian raids–Orkney and the Western Isles (four examples in the Scottish National Museum in Edinburgh)–and in Ireland–fifteen or more in the National Museum in Dublin–where they are characteristic of the Viking cemeteries. From England, which was attacked mostly by the Danes, only one example has been recorded, and that not for certain, from the River Lea at Enfield, near London; a single-edged blade from the Thames at Mortlake is of Norwegian character and may have had one of these hilts. This type lasted from perhaps about 775 to about 900.

Type III has a three-lobed (occasionally five-lobed) pommel, often with zoomorphic ends, and straight guards. The central lobe is always the largest. It is the normal type in north-west Europe during the ninth and tenth centuries, where its main development seems to have taken place in north-western Germany and southern Scandinavia, under the influence of the zoomorphic pommels which were characteristic of this region during the fifth and sixth centuries; it is, in fact, in all its forms simply an enlarged development of the cocked-hat pommels of Type V of the Migration Period. This type is rarely found in the British Isles, though it occurs in Scotland (on the island of Eigg) and in Dublin.

Type IV is perhaps rather a sub-type of III. It has an almost flat pommel with five lobes, generally all of the same size; the lower edges are usually straight, as are the guards, but occasionally both are slightly curved. The distribution of the type is wide: many were found in graves at Knin and elsewhere in Jugoslavia; some in Norway (one with a curved pommel-base and guard) and others in Ireland, and one magnificently decorated pommel of nielloed silver was found in Fetter Lane in London. This is in the British Museum. Also in London (in the Wallace Collection, in Manchester Square) is another, but it was acquired in France and was probably found there. This sword is of great importance, for on the under surface of the lower hilt is engraved the name HILTIPREHT. This may refer to an owner, but it is more likely to be a maker, for there is a similar sword of the same type in the National Museum of Ireland in Dublin.[5] This type is generally held to be Frankish, though the Fetter Lane example may suggest an English influence upon the development of a Viking type; it was in use between about 850 and 950.

Type V is a distinctive group, dating between about A.D. 875 and 950, with a very high peaked central lobe and sharply curved pommel-base and guards. One from the River Thames at Wallingford (from which the type has been named) and others found in Norway bear English ornament (in the 'Trewhiddle' style)[6] of late ninth century date. This, combined with the fact that more have been found in England than anywhere else, suggests very strongly that it is a native English type.

Type VI may equally well be said to be a Danish type of the tenth and early eleventh centuries, for its greatest concentration of finds seems to be in Denmark and those parts of England where the Danes under Sweyn Forkbeard and Knut were concentrated upon London and south-east England during the first quarter of the eleventh century. Most, in fact, have come out of the Thames. The type is lacking in Scotland and Ireland, and its main concentration in Europe is to be found in the south and east of the Baltic.

Some of Type VII have an almost semi-circular, flattish pommel in the shape of a tea-cosy. Most examples have grooves or beaded lines which divide the surface into three parts, vestiges of the threefold division characteristic of the pommels of Types III and VI, though many have only one horizontal groove, suggesting a division between pommel and upper guard, and some have none at all. It is found in fairly wide distribution, and its associations in Scandinavia suggest that it

4

belongs mainly to the tenth century. Many examples have been found in rivers along the western coasts of France; there is a particularly fine one from the Scheldt in the Royal Armouries, and another in the same collection from the Thames at Bray. There are two in the Museum at York, found in the city–which was captured by the Danes in 867–and another in the British Museum, from the River Lea at Edmonton in London, and others–one complete with its scabbard and grip– from the Seine at Paris, relics probably of the great siege of 885–6.

The last two types are transitional forms which link the Viking sword, with its generally short guard and lobated pommel, with the later medieval sword, the knightly weapon of the Age of Chivalry. Type VIII has a much simplified development of Type VI. The divisions between the upper and lower parts have vanished, as well as the lobes, leaving a form just like a Brazil nut. Nearly all swords with this form of pommel have slender guards, much longer than the usual Viking ones and often curved towards the blade. The Vikings called this form of hilt *gaddhjalt*, spike-hilt. The earliest swords with these hilts have been found in Norwegian burials of about A.D. 950, and its latest forms may perhaps belong to the tenth century. Its distribution (in its earlier form within the Viking Period) tended to be confined to northern and central Europe, with isolated examples in Norway. One was found near the city of Ely, Cambridgeshire.[7]

Type IX is a bye-form of VIII. The general shape of the hilt is similar, but the pommel at first retains the division into upper and lower parts, the upper part taking on an exaggerated cocked hat form. It is much less common than Type VIII, and one cannot say that it is found more in one locality than another, for only isolated examples have been found, widely separated. Its greatest popularity, in a more massive form, was in Germany during the 13th century.

There is one further pommel-type, which can be included in the latest of the Viking hilt-styles. This is in the form of a thick disc, sometimes with the edges bevelled off. Now in nearly every work in any language which discussed medieval swords, you will come across statements such as 'The disc-shaped pommel did not come into use until the twelfth century'. There is pictorial evidence to show that this is quite wrong; it was used in the eleventh and even in the tenth century, but archaeological support was lacking until about 1950, when a series of late Viking graves–dating between 1000 and 1100–was opened in Finland. In these graves were found a number of swords with disc pommels, a discovery which enables us to say with certainty that this, the most common type of medieval sword-pommel, popular right up to about 1550, was in use by about 1050.[8]

The Viking swords give the impression that their decoration was wrought by the sword-smith, not by a jeweller. In nine cases out of ten, it consists of simple designs applied to the iron in various ways; in the earlier part of the period, a thick plating of silver, often covered all over with small punched dots or crosses or small geometrical figures, was popular; during the ninth and tenth centuries, this plating was often engraved with running interlace patterns of the kind used in book decoration (the Lindisfarne Gospels, for instance) and engraved runic stones to which niello was sometimes applied. Toward the period's end, we find geometrical patterns inlaid in brass, on a background of tin, each figure outlined by a strip of copper wire. A simple and much-used decoration all through the period consisted of the whole surface being covered with closely placed vertical strips of copper and tin alternately, running from edge to edge of each element. This was sometimes elaborated by little herringbone patterns inlaid between each vertical strip, in a different metal. These decorations are often finely executed, works of real craftsmanship which in its way is far more effective than the older jeweller's work, for the direct simplicity of the ornament is well-matched to the grim dignity of the sword's shape.

The plating was applied to these hilts by hammering or burnishing thin sheets of gold, silver, copper, brass or tin foil onto the surface of the iron, which was covered all over with a close network of fine cuts; the softer metal of the plating was forced into these cuts and held securely. In some cases where plating was decorated with interlace or other patterns by geometrical designs, the ground would be of tin or silver, the pattern itself of brass or gold outlined with copper or bronze. Sometimes the pattern was not inlaid in metal but filled with black niello.[9]

The swords of Type V, probably Anglo-Saxon, have decoration applied in thick embossed or engraved plates of silver or bronze; one or two have been found with medallions like coins (but not actual coins) inlaid in the centre of the pommel. Some Type IV swords have a quite different sort of decoration, like sprays of foliage; this is a typically Frankish ornament of the ninth and tenth centuries, and strengthens the supposition that such swords are of a Frankish fashion.

All of these hilt-forms are logical developments of the styles of the Migration Period. In a sword with a 7th century hilt from Valsgarde in Sweden can be seen the same basic shape of the lower guard and the upper guard (or pommel-bar) with the pommel on top. Though more massively made, and no longer using the riveted sandwich method of making the lower and upper guards, the now nonfunctional rivet-heads are often still present. The most characteristic Viking pommel is made of three lobes, upon which basic form there is an infinity of variation. These later hilts were heavier and more solid than the earlier ones–they needed to be, to balance the bigger and heavier blades which had come into use circa 800.

The question of blades is complex because the actual form, once it was set, varies little. Most blades from that time on had various names, slogans or patterns inlaid upon them in iron, gold, silver, and brass (latten), and these inlays themselves present us with such fascinating variations that they deserve a detailed study.[10]

In considering the blades of the swords used by the Vikings and their contemporaries, three factors have to be taken into account–their form, their manufacture and distribution, but above all, the inscriptions which were inlaid into their surfaces–which are much varied as to their style and content, and the symbolism which many of them represent is quite incomprehensible to us in the 21st century.[11]

Confusion is added to the complexity when we observe the fact that, while some swords of the Migration Period were handed on to succeeding generations, often being in use for a century or more, the majority were either placed in great massed deposits like those found in the Danish bogs at Vimose, Nydam, Thorsbjerg, and Kragebul or put into the burial-mounds of their owners. Even here they did not always rest in peace, for they might be taken out by a later member of the dead man's family (as the resolute girl Hervor opened her father's mound and forced his ferocious ghost to give her the family sword Tyrfing) or looted by a marauding Viking like Skeggi of Midfirth in Iceland, who broke into the howe of the 7th century Danish King Hrolf Kraki and took his sword, handing it on to his family so that it had a second lifetime of some 150 years. We have seen, too, how some swords were destroyed by burning or being bent into weird, twisted shapes or by being broken into pieces (as were those which Dr. Leppäaho found in those Viking graves in Finland). Some, like Skofnung and others which now rest in private collections or museums, must have been put into the grave well covered up and protected, because so many of them survived to this day in good, even usable, condition. There is still the question as to why they were buried with the dead in the first place.

The blades in use during the Migration Period were not beautiful in form, however gorgeous they may have looked when new by reason of the splendid patterns produced by the complex and mysterious method of forging by pattern-welding. Their outline was very plain, the edges running almost parallel to a rounded point. They are clumsy to handle, too, for the point of balance is nearer to the point than to the hilt, which makes them seem slow and heavy in the hand. At some time, which archaeological discoveries give us reason to believe was around the turn of the 8th and 9th centuries, much stouter, broader, heavier blades began to be produced. These, being heavier, feel even more clumsy. Then, about a hundred years later, the blade-form which was to become the beautiful knightly sword of the Age of Chivalry and was to continue as the broadsword of the 16th, 17th and 18th centuries began emerging from the forges of a blade-maker in the Rhineland. These blades were, on the average, a little longer than their predecessors, but their main difference was that they tapered elegantly towards a moderately sharp point. In some, the taper widened quite strongly just below the hilt. This altered shape gave the sword the final touch of quality which lasted until the end of its days. This sword can be wholeheartedly admired without sentimentality about its romantic aspect or revulsion at its function. Here is the very essence of beauty–austere perfection of line and proportion, the three elements of blade, guard and pommel forming a harmoniously balanced whole which need not suffer in comparison with any other art form. It is obvious that these swords and their successors have much in common, as art forms, with the severe purity of the Chinese porcelain of the Sung dynasty. Be that as it may, this handsome aspect is something of a bonus when it is added to the fact that the sword was so closely associated with much of what was most significant in a man's life–family ties, loyalty, valour in the excitement of combat, and the last funeral rites. A man was never parted from it; he carried it in the king's hall and on all social occasions. It hung at his back when he was at table and by his bed while he slept–it was indeed his 'shoulder-companion'. We can appreciate the lament of the poet Bersi the Dueller, a famous swordsman (an archetypal D'Artagnan) of the tenth century, when he declared that when he could no longer wield his sword, life would hold nothing more for him.

> *'The trolls may have my life when I can no longer redden keen Laufi.*
> *Then you may carry the destroyer of the mailshirt into the howe.'*

These blades have their point of balance very much nearer to the hilt, giving then a swift mobility without in any way lessening their tremendous striking power. Forty years ago, *The Archaeology of Weapons* compared the agility of these swords as against their predecessors with the speed and manoeuvrability of a fighter aircraft of the 1940s with the slow movements of a biplane of 1917.

We can only make guesses, some inspired, some absurd, as to where the pattern-welded blades were made, but when we come to the 'new' blades of the 9th–10th centuries, we are on surer ground. A great number which have survived and been examined are found to have a name inlaid, in large letters of iron, in the broad shallow fuller of the blades. This name, **UFLBERHT**, can be said with some confidence to be Frankish and to originate somewhere in the region of the Middle Rhine. The town of Solingen grew up here, from which fine sword-blades came all through the Middle Ages and down to our time. Another source of blades, maybe for an even longer period, is the ancient Noricum, from where the Romans and their adversaries in Western Europe got their blades. This is now pin-pointed by the town of Passau on the Upper Danube, from which fine blades were exported all over the known world.

Though Ulfberht is the name of a Frankish bladesmith, no one man could possibly have made all the Ulfberht blades, for the earliest to be found in dateable contexts are of the years around 850,

Fig. 2. Blade fragment from grave 1 at Valkeakoski (formerly Sääksmäki), Rapola, Finland, NM2767, with an **+VLFBERH+** damascened (pattern-welded) iron inlaid inscription within the 2.4 cm wide fuller upon one side and **IIIC✤ƆIII** on the opposite face. See Jorma Leppäaho, *Späteisenzeitliche Waffen aus Finnland: Schwertinschriften und Waffenverzierungen des 9.–12. Jahrhunderts* (Helsinki, 1964), pp. 36–37. Photographs courtesy of and copyright National Museum of Finland, negative 28039 (upper) and 28038 (lower).

and the latest found in early 12th century graves may have been made decades earlier than the time of their burial; and even though many survive, one man in a long working life could not have made them all–even those which survive. But how long was a working life for a skilled craftsman? The average expectation in the 10th century was about 35 years; and for every Ulfberht blade which survives, literally hundreds must have been made. Thus, hundreds of blades over a period of 250 years is a great many blades. So Ulfberht may have been a smith, but he obviously was the founder and President of Ulfberht, Ltd., which as a company long outlasted him.

A rival firm seems to have set up during the 10th century, because after circa 925, swords have been found in dateable graves bearing, in the same technique of inlaid strips of iron, the name **INGELRI**. One of the first blades by this maker to be found and identified (it was in a lake at Sigridsholm in Sweden) had the words **ME FECIT**[12] (made me) following the name, leaving no doubt that these inlaid names were the names of makers, not owners. So far there are not so many of these as Ulfberhts, but that means only that not so many have been recovered from the ground and identified (by means of x-ray, or sharp eyesight), there are no doubt many still waiting to be found today (or tomorrow), which is always a cheering thought for the lover and collector of such things.

One or two other swords have come to light bearing similar smith-names, but none in such great numbers as Ulfberhts and Ingelris. Therefore it is perhaps possible to say that in these we have the work of an individual smith. These rare survivors are, so far, identified as follows:

NISOMEFECIT (3 swords)
BANTO (1)
ATALBALD (1)
LEUTFRIT (2)

BENNO (1)

EROLT (1)

INNO (1 sword–and this is a name, not part of **INNOMINEDOMINI**, for it is followed by **ME FECIT**)

GECELIN ME FECIT (8 swords)

The Ulfberht inscriptions are characterized by the insertion of a cross among the letters– **+ULFBERH+T**, and never (as so far observed) have they added Me Fecit. The Ingelri blades sometimes, but not always, have a plain cross preceding the name and sometimes, but not always, Me Fecit after. The blades of both these workshops have groups of various symbols on their reverse sides which appear to be arranged in an infinite variety of ways and which undoubtedly meant something in the 10th century which is completely hidden from us now. The same group of symbols is on the reverse of the Niso, Atalbald, Banto, Benno, Inno, and Erolt blades, and their variants seem to have been standard. The Gicelin blades, however, are quite different. The technique of inlaying the lettering with strips of iron wire is the same, but in all the eight survivors, the fullers are narrower, and the letters neater. The name is preceded and followed by a cross, a few plain but most crutched, and in all of them the reverse bears the entirely Christian invocation **IN NOMINE DOMINI** (In the name of the Lord).

The find places of all of these swords are widely distributed, all over northwestern Europe, so while we may not say that one kind is Swedish and another West German, we can see that they went all over the map–as indeed the warriors who carried them did. The two Leutfrit blades are a case in point. One was found in southern Russia and the other in the River Witham near Lincoln.

The 'new' type of blades was only fractionally lighter than the earlier ones, sometimes (like the Leutfrit sword from Lincoln) they were actually heavier, but because the point of balance is so

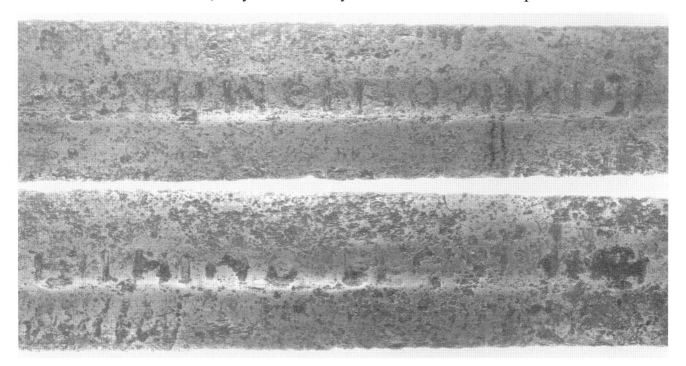

Fig. 3. Iron inlaid inscriptions, variations upon *In Nomine Domini*, upon the forte of an eleventh century blade, reading **✠INIMOFEIOMINI✠** above and **✠INIMOIEEC** ... **NI✠** below. Note that the fuller is narrower than that of the earlier sword in fig. 2, but that the iron inlaid inscriptions are confined to the fuller width in both cases. This sword has a disc pommel and had fractured just beyond the area of the inscriptions. Photograph by Doug Whitman.

much nearer to the hand that wields them, they feel lighter. A feature which appears now for the first time is one which lasted as long as sword-blades have been made: the tang and the upper part of blade, sometimes only about 4 cm and sometimes as much as 12 cm of it, were made of a softer, less carbonized metal. This part was scarf-welded onto the main, tempered, business part of the blade, making it less liable to fracture at the hilt. This scarf weld may often be seen on blades, though it depends upon the kind of etching effect which mud or earth or atmosphere has had upon a blade.

The most significant exposure of blade inscriptions of the 20th century, with the most far-reaching effects which are only just beginning to be felt, is in the posthumously published work of Dr. Jorma Leppäaho of Helsinki University. In the late 1940s and early 1950s, he cleared a number of graves of the late Viking period, in Southern Finland. The first surprising fact which he noted was that on many of these swords, the pommels were not of the usual 'Viking' styles, but were of the thick disc form always previously associated only with the 13th and 14th and 15th centuries. Now here they were, indisputably of the 11th! Some were of plain disc form, others of what has come to be called the 'wheel' form, where the disc is very thick with the edges strongly bevelled to leave a circular boss in the centre of the disc, like the nave of a wheel. One of these wheel pommels was faceted, in a way often seen in German sculpture of the later 14th century. There are many surviving swords with this kind of pommel, which have always been considered by students of arms–myself among them–to be no earlier than circa 1325. Now we have to reconsider one of our verdicts upon them, for they may turn out to be two centuries earlier than we thought. Among these wheel pommels, however, there was none having the central boss recessed, nor with the bevelled edges of a concave section.[13]

The most startling and significant discoveries, however, did not come until the blades of these swords–some only fragments–were examined by the applications of chemistry and by taking x-ray photographs. These experiments showed that, along with the 'old' iron inlaid inscriptions were others of a quite different kind, inlaid in gold, silver, or brass (latten) wires. As with the wheel pommels, before the illustration and publication of these experiments in 1964, nobody would have dared to suggest that they were any earlier than the late 12th century at the very earliest; most would have been assigned to the late 13th or 14th centuries. In consequence, again, we have to reassess our statements (and indeed, ought to re-label a lot of swords in the great museums).

Overriding enthusiasm for the sword may give the impression that no other weapons were much regarded, or much used, by the Vikings and their predecessors. This would be quite wrong, for axe, spear, and sax (a short single-edged weapon rather like a Khyber knife) were very often used, particularly in battles; and they, too, had their splendid names, 'the flying dragon of the fight' (spear) for instance, or 'witch of the shield' (axe). But it was the sword they sang about, boasted about, and dreamed about. It was the weapon par excellence, too, of their great favourite occupation, the duel. The carefully worked-out rules of the duel were in full use by the eighth century, and in their formality, they seem to have been far more strict than the rules governing duelling in the 16th and 17th centuries and even in the 18th, when the matter was far more formal.

In the work of Saxo Grammaticus he says:

> For of old, in the ordering of combats, men did not try to exchange their blows thick and fast; but there was a pause, and at the same time a definite succession in striking; the contest being carried on with few strokes, but those terrible, so that honour was paid more to the mightiness than to the number of the blows.[14]

There were two kinds of duel, an informal one called 'Einvigi', in which there were few rules, and a most punctilious formal one called 'Holmgang'. This means literally 'going on an island', and whenever possible, such duels were fought on small islets, but where this was not possible, a space like a boxing ring, and much the same size, was marked out on the ground. These Holmgang duels were often used as means of settling disputes about property or women, like the later Trial by Combat. They were much abused, though, by tough characters like professional duellists and Berserks to get possession of someone's wife, or his land, or even just his loose property, or sometimes–like Bersi the Dueller, of whom we read in Kormac's Saga–just for the hell of it. In Kormac's Saga, we find one of the best descriptions of the Holmganga law. Kormac borrowed Skofnung from Skeggi of Midfirth for his duel. Here is what happened:

> A cloak was spread under their feet. Bersi said 'You Kormac, challenged me to Holmganga; but instead of it I offer you Einvigi. You are young and inexperienced, and at Holmganga there are difficult rules, but none whatever at Einvigi!' Kormac answered, 'I shan't fight better at Einvigi, and I'll risk it, and be on equal footing with you in everything.' 'You shall have your way, then,' said Bersi.

> This was the Holmganga law: that the cloak should be ten feet from one end to the other, with loops should be put pegs with a head at the top. These were called Tjosnur. Then three squares, their sides each a foot beyond the other, must be marked round the cloak. Outside the squares must be placed four poles called Hoslur (hazel poles). It was called a Hazelled Field when it was prepared thus. Each man must have three shields, and when these were made useless he must stand upon the cloak, even if he had moved out of it before, and defend himself with his weapons.

> He who had been challenged must strike first. If either was wounded so that blood came upon the cloak he was not obliged to fight any longer. If either stepped with one of his feet outside the hazel poles he was held to have retreated; if he stepped outside with both feet he was held to have fled. One man was to hold the shield before each of the combatants. The one who received the most wounds was to pay a Holmslausn (indemnity for being released from the fight) of three marks of silver.

> Thorgils held the shield for his brother, and Thord Arnidsaron that of Bersi, who struck the first blow and cleft Kormac's shield. Kormac struck at Bersi in the same way. Each of them spoiled three shields for the other. Then Kormac had to strike; he struck, and Bersi parried with Hviting. Skofnung cut off its point, and it fell on Kormac's hand and wounded him in the thumb, whose joint was rent so that blood fell on the cloak. Thereupon the others intervened and did not want them to go on fighting. Kormac said, 'It's not much of a victory Bersi has got from my accident, though we part now.'[15]

So some fights, like the one of Bersi v. Kormac, were well-regulated affairs where nobody came to much harm. (In this fight the only damage was that Bersi's sword, Hviting, was broken, Kormac's Skofnung–which he had borrowed from Skeggi–got a nasty nick in it and Kormac got a cut thumb.) Very different was one fought by Egil, described in Egil's Saga.

> There was a fine field not far from the sea, where the Holmganga was to be. There the place was marked out by a ring of stones. Ljot came thither with his men, prepared for the Holmganga with shield and sword. He was very large and strong, and when he arrived on the field at the Holmgang place the Berserk frenzy came upon him, and he howled fiercely and bit the rim of his shield.

> Egil made ready for the Holmganga, having his old shield, with his sword Nadr girt to his side and with Dragvandil (his other sword) in his hand. He went inside the marks of the

duelling place (i.e. the spaces marked out round the cloak) but Ljot was not ready. Egil raised his sword and sang.

After the song, Ljot came forward and pronounced the laws of the Holmganga, that whoever stepped outside the stones which are set around the place of the Holmganga should ever afterwards be called Nithing (coward).

Then they rushed at each other, and Egil struck at Ljot, who covered himself with his shield while Egil dealt blow after blow so that Ljot could not strike back. He drew back to get room to swing his sword, but Egil went just as fast after him and smote most violently. Ljot went out beyond the mark-stones and to and fro on the field. Thus went the first attack. Then Ljot asked to be allowed to rest, which Egil granted.

Egil bade Ljot to make himself ready: 'I want this fought out,' he said. Ljot sprang to his feet, and Egil ran forward at once and struck him; he went so close that Ljot stepped back, and his shield did not cover him. Then Egil smote him above the knee and cut off his leg. Ljot fell, and at once died.

Another story concerning a fight is very different again. It is a tale of two peaceable men, farmers from Iceland, Thorstein and Bjarni. Neither of them was quarrelsome, but one of Bjarni's men was rude to Thorstein. He took no notice, but his tough old father who had been a fighter in his youth, insisted that Thorstein had been insulted and that he must fight Bjarni. So in the end Bjarni walked over to Thorstein's farm:

'Thorstein, today you'll have to come out and fight with me, in the meadow here.' Thorstein wasn't willing, but in the end he went and fetched his weapons and they fought with swords until their shields were cut to pieces. Then Bjarni said he was thirsty, so Thorstein told him to go and get a drink in the brook. Bjarni laid his sword down and went off. Thorstein had a good look at it while Bajarni was gone, and when he came back they fought again, and each found the other a good opponent. Then Bjarni said his shoe was undone, and Thorstein told him to do it up. While Bjarni was doing this, Thorstein went back into the house and brought out two fresh shields and another sword for Bjarni, which, he said, was less blunt than the one he had been using. At the same time he said he'd be very willing to stop fighting and come to terms. However, Bjarni said no, they must go on, but Thorstein refused to strike the opening blow. Then Bjarni cut Thorstein's shield clean away, but Thorstein hewed through Bjarni's shield in return. 'That was a mighty stroke' said Bjarni. 'No better than yours,' said Thorstein.

Again Thorstein offered to come to terms. Now they had no shields to protect them, and as Bjarni was about to strike, he thought better of it, and said they had done enough. The end of the story was that Bjarni put in a man to manage the farm for Thorstein's old father and took Thorstein into his household, and they remained close friends all their lives.'

Here we capture the very atmosphere of the Einvigi. Very different is the talk of another fight, this time a real free-for-all, a small battle between two groups of men. There is a splendid description of it in Eyrbryggja Saga, a fight on the ice on a river between Steinthor and his friends against the sons of Thorbrand. These latter defended themselves on a rock skerry rising out of the ice:

…And when they had been contending against each other for a good while, Thord Hawkeye made a run at the skerry and hurled a spear at Thorleif kimbi; for he was ever in the forefront of the battle. The missile struck Thorleif's shield, and Thord was so busy defending himself that he lost his footing on the sheet of ice and fell on his back and slid backwards off the skerry. Thorleif kimbi sprang after him and was going to slay him before he got to his feet again, but Steinthor ran up and defended Thord with his shield, and with his other hand he hewed at

Thorleif kimbi and cut off his leg above the knee. At the same time, another man cut at Steinthor's middle, and as he saw this he leapt into the air and the blade came between his legs, performing all three actions at one and the same instant.

It is hardly surprising, in view of this, that Steinthor was said to be one of the finest fighting men in Iceland.

There are numerous tales to tell of the deeds of the Vikings, tales funny, tales bloody, tales hard to believe but probably true. There are the ferocious Shield-Maidens, not mythical Valkyrs but real girls of the same kind as the fighting Maharanees of the Rajputs in India.

To return to the sword in the river or in the grave. Why?

That the dead man wanted to take his sword with him to wherever he thought he was going is probably totally irrelevant. Really the Song of Roland–a Viking epic in its own right–says it all. 'Let no man have you who would run before another'. In the Age of the Vikings, and long after, there were three ways of ensuring this. One was to destroy the sword altogether by breaking it in pieces or by bending and twisting it up so that it could not be used at all. Another was by carefully wrapping it up and putting it in the grave with him in the expectation that somebody would come and take it out of the grave–as Skeggi of Midfirth did when he raided the grave at Roskilde of the 7th century Hrolf Kraki, or when the girl Hervor took Tyrfing out of her father's grave to give to her son Grettir. Another, perhaps, more usual way was to follow the age-old tradition of the Norman people–the Celts in particular–and throw a sword into the water of a lake or river (to the great advantage of 20th century researchers).

> The Count struggles to his feet; he tries to break Durendal on a dark stone which stands there. Ten times he strikes, but the sword will not splinter nor break. 'Eh, good Durendal, you were set for sorrow. So long have you been wielded by a good vassal. Now I am lost and can care for you no longer. I have fought so many on the field with you, and kept down so many countries which Charles holds, whose beard is white. Let no man have you who would run before another!' Again Roland struck the sword on the stone. The steel grates, but will not splinter or break. When he sees that he cannot break it at all, he begins to mourn the sword to himself. 'Eh! Good Durendal, how beautiful you are, how bright and white! How you gleam and flash in the sunlight!'

Nor is it surprising, from what we know of the difficulties of its making, that a certain mystery hung over the creation of a good sword, and that poets associated such weapons with gods and giants and long-dead heroes of the past. From what we know also of the complex ritual of duelling and the skill of good swordsmanship, it is only to be expected that a vast body of sword-lore–part technicalities and part superstition–grew up, a small portion of which has survived, and an even smaller portion of which is comprehensible to us now. The conditions of society changed in time, and a more settled existence replaced the old heroic way of life of the warrior lord and his band of followers. Still the value of the sword as a weapon remained of sufficient importance to keep its reputation alive. Heroic tales continued to be told, based on a world of adventure in which the sword in the hero's hand was the key to achievement. In medieval times it gained fresh glories as the weapon of the Christian knight, and for a long while duelling customs kept up the necessity for swordsmanship. Now it is obsolete, and we can catch only the reflection of its former splendour in the literature of the past. There is no single object among the possessions of a modern man which may be compared to it. It demands, therefore, a determined effort of study and imagination if we are to realize the significance of the sword, so powerful a weapon in men's hands and so potent a symbol in men's minds for hundreds of years. But such an effort is indeed worth while, for much of the life and vigour of our early literature must be lost for ever when the memory of the sword has faded.[16]

Such is the sentiment and the mystique. To originate and sustain that, the work of generations of fine craftsmen was needed. In this book a few good examples of this craftsmanship are calibrated. When they are reassessed not with the eye alone, but with the shaping spirit of the imagination, understanding may come.

[1] H.R. Ellis Davidson, *The Sword in Anglo-Saxon England* (Oxford, 1962). A Fragment from an Estonian Viking Epic, *Kalevapoeg*.

[2] Davidson (1962), p. 214.

[3] Heribert Seitz, *Blankwaffen I: Geschichte und Typenentwicklung im europäischen Kulturbereich Von der prähistorischen Zeit bis zum Ende des 16. Jahrhunderts* (Braunschveig, 1964).

[4] Jan Petersen, *De Norske Vikingesverd* (Oslo, 1919) and A. N. Kirpichnikov, *Russische Waffen des 9–15th Jahrhunderts.*

[5] Dublin, The National Museum of Ireland.

[6] Seitz (1964); the finest example of the hilt-form is the Gilling West sword in York.

[7] This is in the Museum of Archaeology and Anthropology in Downing College, Cambridge.

[8] Jorma Leppäaho, *Späteisenzeitliche Waffen aus Finnland: Schwertinschriften und Waffenverzierungen des 9.–12. Jahrhunderts* (Helsinki, 1964).

[9] This is generally referred to as the Ringerika Style.

[10] Leppäaho (1964).

[11] Ewart Oakeshott, 'Beati Omnipotensque Angeli Christi', *Park Lane Arms Fair Catalogue* 3 (1986), pp. 5–14.

[12] Seitz (1964), pl. 63, p. 106.

[13] Leppäaho (1964).

[14] Davidson (1962), p. 196.

[15] Davidson (1962), p. 266 and R. Ewart Oakeshott, *The Archaeology of Weapons* (London, 1960), pp. 155–156.

[16] Davidson (1962), pp.215–216.

Portions of this chapter are excerpted from Ewart Oakeshott, 'Medieval Swords–Part IV: Odin's Flame', *The Gun Report*, vol. XXXI, no. 8 (Jan., 1986), pp. 18–23 and Ewart Oakeshott, 'Medieval Swords–Part V: Destroyer of the Mail Shirt', *The Gun Report*, vol. XXXI, no. 9 (Feb., 1986), pp. 14–19, courtesy of World-Wide Gun Report, Inc., P.O. Box 38; Aledo, IL 61321. The entire series of *Gun Report* articles has been reprinted in a single volume as *Sword in Hand* (Minneapolis, 2000) and is available from Arms & Armor, Inc., 1101 Stinson Blvd. NE; Minneapolis, MN 55413.

Overview of Hilt & Blade Classifications
Lee A. Jones

The swords of the Viking Age have traditionally been classified on the basis of the form and decoration of their hilts, as this is where the variation is greatest and the developmental relationships are the most obvious. Subtle evolution of blade form may also be discerned during this period, but this is generally gradual and rarely offers convenient 'break points' for natural typological classification. Preferred blade length and weight would have varied among warriors throughout the period, as men vary in their own attributes, and this contemporary variation obscures recognition of overall trends in blade dimensions. Also, the manufacture of blades was likely limited to relatively fewer centres of production than that of hilts, with consequently increased standardization. While particular styles of hilt are often associated with corresponding types of blade, this frequently is not the case. Some blades appear to have had a long 'working' life, as an earlier blade is occasionally found mounted with a style of hilt which clearly had yet to be devised when the blade was forged.

Classifications Based Upon Hilts

At first glance, there appears to be a near limitless variety of forms of Viking Age sword hilt, and indeed, as handmade objects, no two are exactly alike. After some consideration, however, it may be seen that, among swords in general, those of the Viking Age are all relatively similar, having symmetrical single-handed grips, a simple crossguard or lower guard and an upper hilt composed of an upper guard and or pommel. Perfect schemes of classification are rarely, if ever, achieved. Fortunately, this is inconsequential as the ultimate value of a typological classification lies not in it being an end unto itself, but in being a tool with which to organize recognition of common features and thus relationships. For the swords of the Viking Age, Jan Petersen's classification centred upon the Norwegian material and published in 1919[1] has proven most enduring. The same work also presents classifications of Viking Age spears and axes and proposes a still well accepted chronology based upon associations between the various types and other dateable artefacts found within excavated graves. Petersen has assigned letter designations, A to Æ, to the main hilt styles, with the earliest types being assigned the letters at the front of the alphabet and the latest those at the end. Petersen placed those types less common in his experience or otherwise not fitting into the main classification into *særtyper* or 'distinctive types' and placed them in his book in sections at the close of each century's main types. R.E.M. Wheeler published a somewhat simpler classification, more focused upon the British material, in 1927[2] which Ewart Oakeshott subsequently expanded in 1960[3] to include two further types and which is presented in the preceding section on pp. 3–5. Alfred Geibig published a multiaxial scheme in 1991[4] which covers the material of western Germany. Both Wheeler and Geibig omit some of the forms described by Petersen and include other forms not presented in Petersen's system, owing primarily to the differences in geographical focus between their works. Still further forms are described in the works of those scholars such as A.N. Kirpichnikov[5] and Leena Tomanterä[6] who have concentrated on finds from further eastern localities.

Jakobsson[7] divided the majority of hilt styles into six design principles. The first three incorporate triangular pommels, three lobed pommels and five lobed pommels, roughly corresponding to Wheeler's types II, III and IV, respectively. Jakobsson's design principle 4 is the absence of a pommel with retention of the upper guard and corresponds to Wheeler's type I. Jakobsson's fifth design principle is the use of a curved lower guard, which incorporates Wheeler's types V through VII, while his sixth design principle is the opposite of the fourth, with the presence of a pommel and the absence of an upper guard. Even a classification so simplified as Jakobsson's faces confounding examples. Curved crossguards may be associated with hilts having both a pommel and an upper guard or with hilts lacking either the pommel or upper guard. Some of Petersen's types allow for either three or five lobed pommels on the basis of otherwise striking similarities and both Wheeler and Jakobsson acknowledged that a case could be made for combining these types into a single 'lobated' type.[8]

Plotting swords of known find place on maps by type, which Jakobsson[9] has done for his own and Petersen's types, leads to the inescapable conclusion that these swords did travel far and wide. Indeed the diversity of origins and styles of swords present in a particular Viking community must likely be analogous to the diversity of origins and styles of automobiles or watches which would be encountered analysing a modern community. The craftsmen who made these hilts were not constrained by twentieth century classifications and, though surely there were traditions to be maintained, it is clear that fashions did change and attractive features noticed on a sword hilt imported from far afield could soon find their way into local production. Similarly, very old design features frequently persist, often from well back into the Migration Period,[10] though sometimes only in vestigial form, such as rivet heads upon the guards or lines inscribed into a late pommel recalling lobes.

Observations on Petersen's Hilt Types

The catalogue of examples, which follows on p. 25, is organized largely after Petersen's types and the features of many of the types are illustrated and discussed in more detail there. Below, on pp. 18–19, is a diagram laying out the principal styles of Viking Age sword hilts under Petersen's classification and including a few common contemporary forms not included by Petersen. Rather than laying these out alphabetically, they have been grouped along the x-axis by similarities, with first consideration given to Jakobsson's six design principles. The convention of Michael Müller-Wille[11] of shading the hilts usually made of or decorated with materials other than iron has been adopted. Finally, these type examples are positioned along the y-axis to depict the chronology of the types between 700 and 1100, with vertical bars indicating the time span with which each is associated. Curved gray arrows indicate those developmental relationships suggested by Petersen.

Petersen considered his first two main types, type A and B, which both incorporate pommels of triangular profile, to be from the time of the transition between the Migration Period and the Viking Age. Type A pommels are thin and triangular and usually without decoration or lobation, although three lobed and even a seven lobed variant have been documented.[12] The faces of type B guards are relatively short in length perpendicular to the blade but high in the dimension of the blade's length and characteristically have a central ridge perpendicular to the blade's length. Type B pommels are basically of triangular form, although a convex curve may be expected along the two free edges not affixed to the upper guard. The pommels and upper guards of type A and B hilts are both directly attached to the tang, as will often be the case with distinctive types 1 and 2 and the Mannheim type.[13] Petersen regarded type C, which appeared at the opening of the ninth century, as being directly derived from type B. Made of plain iron and without applied decoration, the basic overall hilt profile and the ridged, faceted crossguard face of type B is usually retained, but the upper guard and pommel are now fused and made as a single, usually more massive piece, though grooves and facets may recall the former separate elements of upper guard and pommel. Type H was also regarded by Petersen as being derived from type B and remained in style from the onset of the Viking Age, or even slightly earlier, through to the mid-tenth century. Type H was the style most frequently encountered by Petersen, a ranking maintained in Jakobsson's survey. Just over one quarter of the type H swords in Petersen's material were single-edged.[14] Swords of type H are found across northern Europe and have been documented from as far south as Switzerland and Yugoslavia.[15] Petersen notes that the guards of his type H are wide and have an elliptical contour. The width is greatest at the centre of each lateral face from where it tapers towards the plane of the blade at either end and towards the grip and blade, respectively. In the earlier examples, a central ridge line perpendicular to the blade length may be seen, recalling the geometry seen in types B and C.[16] Unlike the plain iron of type B, the exposed surfaces of these type H hilts are usually covered with a soft metal plating of silver, copper and or brass generally in the form of wires in parallel array and often forming geometric patterns with the contrast between the different metals. Another difference from type B is that type H pommels are secured to the upper guard by rivets, rather than being directly attached to the tang. Type I, represented herein by C23127 in Oslo and depicted in pl. VII, retains most of the features of type H, but differs in being characterized by a lower pommel in which the upper edges of the pommel may have a gently concave contour and in having narrower, lower guards.

Lobated pommels represent a stylistic heritage persisting from the Migration Period, with Petersen's distinctive types 1 and 2 and the later described Mannheim type representing the form in the transition to the Viking Age. Petersen regarded distinctive type 1 as a simplification of a Migration Period pattern having a tall middle section and animal heads on the side. The example he illustrated, C19809 from S. Skjønne, Nore, Buskerud, is without applied decoration.[17] Applied decoration is commonly, though not uniformly, seen upon hilts of distinctive type 2. Hilts of the related Mannheim type will frequently be decorated with characteristic applied engraved or embossed strips of bronze. Some of the Mannheim hilts which have such decoration will show little or no lobulation of a fairly smoothly semicircular pommel. Type D comprises a type with distinctively massive decorated hilts incorporating lobated pommels and is from the first half of the ninth century. The guards, pommel and in some examples the grips are formed of iron which is overlaid with bronze or copper over the recessed areas and with silver covering the raised areas. The pommel of a type D hilt is usually attached to the upper guard by rivets. Petersen regarded his type E as being derived from type D and many examples retain the same three lobed pommel profile with the outer lobes vaguely recalling animal heads. However this shape is not the ultimate defining characteristic as Petersen goes on to note that the shape and even the lobation are absent in some examples. What is uniformly present is an array of closely spaced depressions or pits covering the faces of the guards and pommel. In contrast with type D, Petersen notes that the pommels of type E are fastened directly to the tang rather than being riveted to the upper guard.[18]

Mannheim

A

B

C

H

I

G

F

N

X
earlier

X
later

W

U

V

D

E

1

2

△ hilts with overlaid non-ferrous
decoration and non-ferrous hilts

△ plain iron hilts (after Müller-Wille)

Chronology and Principal Styles of Viking Age Sword Hilts under Petersen's Classification

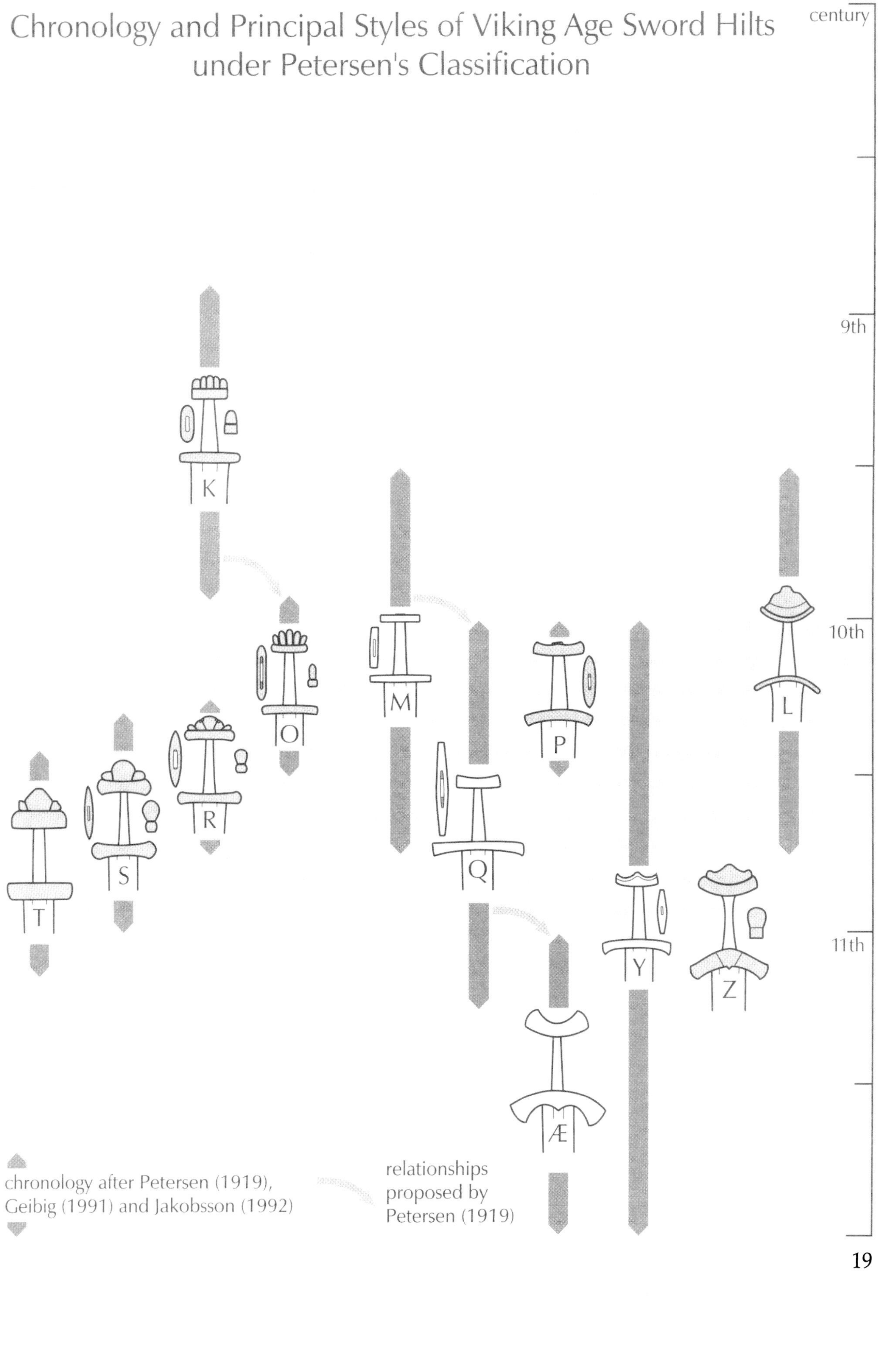

9th

K

10th

M

O

P

L

R

Q

S

T

Y

Z

11th

Æ

chronology after Petersen (1919),
Geibig (1991) and Jakobsson (1992)

relationships
proposed by
Petersen (1919)

19

A number of forms will follow in the tenth century which will retain the legacy of a dominant central pommel lobe and smaller flanking lobes, such as types R, S and T. Other successors to this tradition will be the more semicircular in profile, though still three lobed, pommels of the tenth century types U and V.

Petersen regarded his type K with its characteristic five, and rarely seven, lobed pommel as being native to the Frankish lands by the Rhine and speculated that the type came to Norway in the first half of the ninth century as a result of Viking raids.[19] Find places are broadly distributed across Europe from as far south as the Balkans.[20] The presence of two distinct upper hilt components is most typical of this type; however, in late examples of type K the upper guard and pommel may have fused into a single piece with only incised lines recalling the former boundary, as is the case with C11014 in the Universitetets Oldsaksamling, Oslo, shown on pp. 72–73. Within Norway, the form continued evolving into the second half of the ninth century, ultimately to give rise to type O in the late ninth to early tenth century.

The simplest pattern of Viking Age hilt, type M, has relatively austere bars of iron forming the guards and lacks a pommel. A variable degree of tapering and rounding of the edges of the bars may be expected. Type M is the second most commonly encountered type of Viking hilt and is associated with contexts of the mid ninth century through to the middle of the second half of the tenth century. A variant with gently curving guards, type Q, persists into the early eleventh century, and likely gives rise to type Æ, which has wider and more strongly curved guards which flare out at the ends. The double edged blades associated with type Æ are characterized by Petersen as having a narrow, deep fuller and neither inscriptions nor pattern-welding. The earliest hilt type with guards strongly curved away from the grip, Petersen's type L, has traditionally been regarded as a native English Anglo-Saxon type on the basis of the frequent presence of Anglo-Saxon Trewhiddle style nielloed silver overlay ornament.[21] Also most common in Britain are later forms with similarly curved guards having broader faces, not present within Petersen's classification, but included by Wheeler as his types VI and VII.

Swords having a pommel but lacking an upper guard are typified by type X. Petersen defines two variants of type X collectively dating from the first half of the tenth century through to the middle of the eleventh century. He did not regard the type as being originally Nordic, and noted that it was a common Germanic type in central and northern Europe.[22] More recent finds from outside of Scandinavia suggest the appearance of the type may be as early as the mid ninth century.[23] The rarer form, which Petersen designated as older, has a slimmer and taller pommel, up to 5.1 cm in height, and a crossguard measuring up to 2 cm along the axis of the blade, which may be slightly curved downwards towards the blade. An example of this variant, C26494 in Oslo, may be seen on pp. 116–117. The later and more common of the two variants, typified by the example illustrated on pp. 120–121, has a narrower, lower, 2.7 to 3.5 cm, and thicker pommel and a less thick, 0.7 to 1.4 cm along the axis of the blade, crossguard.[24] Petersen notes that the evolution of pommels towards those smaller in terms of height and width, but thicker, is associated with a lengthening of the crossguard and that the transition to post Viking Age medieval swords may be seen in later examples where the grip side of the pommel assumes a more convex form, such as may be seen in NM 2033:1 on pp. 122–123.

Single-edged Blades of the Viking Age

While the majority of surviving Viking Age swords have double-edged blades, single-edged blades coexisted throughout the period. Petersen[25] describes single-edged blades without surviving hilt elements being found principally in the context of the transition from the Migration Period into

20

the Viking Age. He considered these blades, most often found in western and central Norway, to have 'evolved' locally in that area by stages from the knife length scramasax. With the onset of the Viking Age, the same sort of hilts that are found on double-edged blades began to be applied to these single-edged blades, and in Petersen's material, single-edged blades predominate among swords with hilts of his types C, F and G and are a common finding among types B, H and M. These single-edged blades are often a little longer than contemporaneous double-edged blades, being as much as 80 to 85 cm in length and even rarely exceeding 90 cm. Such single-edged sword blades have traditionally been regarded as the work of local smiths, rather than as being imported products from a specialized workshop. The usual lack of inlays or pattern-welding is offered in defence of this attribution, but occasional exceptions, such as the pattern-welding observed in C24217 in Oslo, illustrated on p. 41, confound either this hypothesis or, more likely, that which holds pattern-welding to be limited to specialized workshops outside of Scandinavia. Single-edged blades also have a reputation of being thicker, and thus heavier, than double-edged blades. From two-dimensional photographs, a balance point well forward from the hilt would be expected, however, the three single-edged swords for which balance points could be measured in preparation for this volume had a balance point located an average of 20% of the length of the blade forward from the cross, as compared with 23% for all measured swords. Single-edged blades are unusual among swords with hilt types appearing after the close of the ninth century. Petersen[26] reported two single-edged blades with hilts of type X from western Norway, noting them to have blades that, while remaining wide, were thinner than those single-edged blades from earlier in the Viking Age.

Double-edged Blades of the Viking Age

Geibig[27] has classified the principal blade forms relevant to the Viking Age into five types on the basis of the length of the blade and fuller, the width of the blade at its origin, the degree of taper of the blade and fuller and the form of the tip. This typology is schematically represented to scale on the following page, with numerical measurement ranges from Geibig's work, in some cases expanded by the swords studied in preparation of this volume, summarized in the table on p. 23.

Blade type 1 carries over from the late Migration Period and persists up to the close of the eighth century. Blade length is moderate, varying between 70 and 80 cm. The type is characterized by moderately wide blades having nearly parallel edges, although a taper to about 86% of the blade's maximum width, measured 60 cm from the origin, is consistent with this type. In a very small measured sample, maximum thickness at the origin ranges between 0.36 and 0.52 cm and tapers to an average 79% of maximum over 60 cm. This average conceals a variation from an essentially flat blade remaining at 98% to another tapering to 69% of thickness. Blades of this type often lack a fuller and have flat faces. Geibig also describes examples with shallow fullers, 1.8 to 2.3 cm in width. The points of type 1 blades are short and spatulate. In the same series of thickness measurements, thickness measured 5 cm back from the tip is 44 to 89% of maximum thickness. These blades are usually pattern-welded, with three, four or occasionally five bands visible on each blade face.

Blade type 2 appears in the mid eighth century and persists until the middle of the tenth century. These blades tend to be slightly longer than their predecessors as well as being slightly wider. The major change, compared with the earlier form, is in degree of taper of the width of the blade, which varies between 67 and 83% of the maximum. Thickness measurements are available on two examples, the first being that illustrated in plate V, with maximums of 0.50 and 0.44 cm, at 60 cm tapering to 82% and 66% of that, respectively, and to 48% and unchanged at 66%, respectively,

Chronology and Principal Styles of Double-Edged Sword Blades of the Viking Age under Geibig's Classification

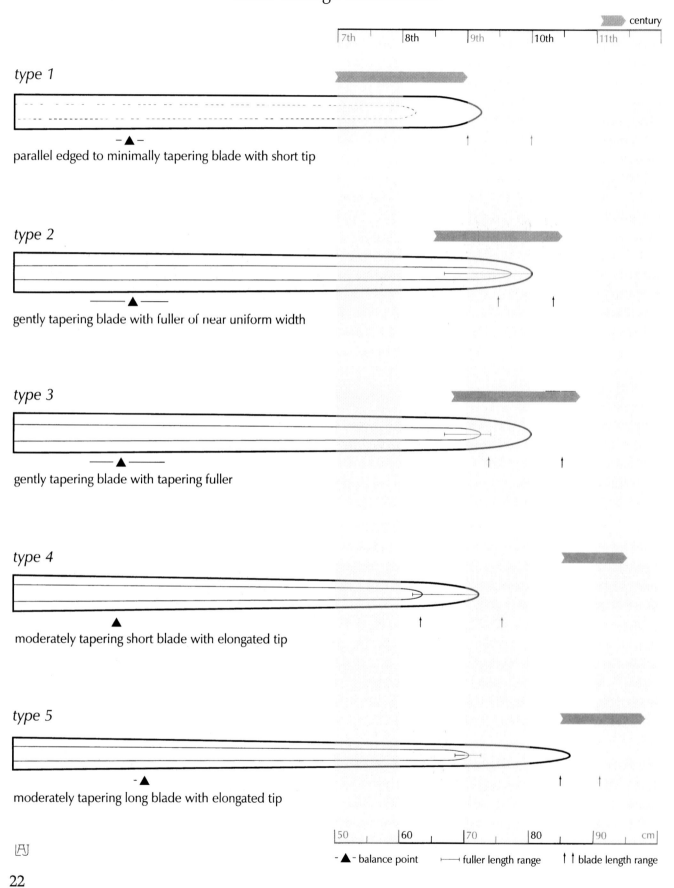

century

7th   8th   9th   10th   11th

type 1

parallel edged to minimally tapering blade with short tip

type 2

gently tapering blade with fuller of near uniform width

type 3

gently tapering blade with tapering fuller

type 4

moderately tapering short blade with elongated tip

type 5

moderately tapering long blade with elongated tip

50   60   70   80   90   cm

- ▲ - balance point   ⊢⊣ fuller length range   ↑ ↑ blade length range

Dimensions of Viking Age Sword Blades in Geibig's Classification

	type 1	type 2	type 3	type 4	type 5
Blade length (cm)	70 - 80	74 - 83	74 - 85	63 - 76	84 - 91
Blade width at origin (cm)	4.4 - 5.8	4.8 - 6.2	5.2 - 5.7	4.5 - 5.0	4.8 - 5.1
Blade taper; width at 60 cm, relative to origin (%)	86 - 93	67 - 83	70 - 82	63 - 67	63 - 81
Fuller length relative to blade length (%)	86	> 83	83 - 93	> 83	79 - 84
Fuller taper; width at 40 cm, relative to origin (%)	94 - 100	95 - 100	80 - 93	73 - 89	78 - 100

Gray blocks highlight the most dramatic changes between the various types.

Some value ranges have been widened from Geibig's work to reflect the swords examined in preparation of this volume

measured 5 cm back from the tips. Fullers are expected in this type, tending to be at least 83% of blade length and with widths generally between 1.7 and 2.7 cm. Measured 40 cm from the origin, the fuller should taper to no less than 95% of its maximum width, this minimal fuller taper being an important distinction between this type of blade and type 3. The transition to the point is more gradual than that of the previous type and may be characterized as being of moderate length. These blades may be pattern-welded, commonly with two or three bands upon each face, and may also bear superimposed iron inlays of geometric form. Non-pattern-welded blades of this form may have iron inlaid Ulfberht or Ingelrii inscriptions. Geibig further subclassifies this type into three variations.

Blade type 3 appears during the second half of the eighth century and continues for two centuries into the second half of the tenth century. The overall size and profile of these blades is very similar to that of type 2 and it is an increased degree of taper of the fuller that most readily sets type 3 apart from type 2. Maximum blade thickness at the forte averaged 0.50 cm with a distribution between 0.38 and 0.61 cm and tapered to an average of 75% at 60 cm and 61% at 5 cm from the tip. Ulfberht inscribed blades may be of this form as may be pattern-welded blades, which also may also bear superimposed iron inlays of geometric form.

Blade type 4 is found in contexts from the mid tenth century through to about the mid eleventh century. Blades of this form tend to be shorter than those of their predecessors, though the extremes of the length distributions overlap somewhat between types. Similarly this group is the narrowest in width at the origin. Geibig reported a maximum width of 5 cm, which would, if seriously enforced, exclude a few otherwise qualifying examples such as the sword in the British Museum, shown on pp. 80–81, from the Thames at King's Reach with an iron inlaid Ingelrii inscription. As a group, these blades are the most strongly tapered of the Viking Age, a distinction that is largely real and only partially resulting from mathematical exaggeration consequent to their shortness and perhaps the potential artifact of the transition to the tip beginning at a distance less than the 60 cm at which taper has been measured. The degree of taper of the fuller also reaches its maximum in this type, likely paralleling the increased taper of the blade. The transition to the tip is longer in this type than in any of the previous types. Ingelrii inscriptions are frequently found on blades of this type and, despite the late dates, blades of this geometry may also be pattern-welded.

Blade type 5 originates in the mid tenth century and continues into the last half of the eleventh century. The longest double-edged blades of the Viking Age fall into this type, which has a moderate width at the origin, usually close to 5 cm. The profile is very much a stretched out version of the previous type, with some examples matching the maximum reduction to 61% of width at 60 cm of type 4. The least tapered examples of type 5 have only a few more percentage points of taper than the least tapered examples of types 2 and 3. Measurements of one example of this type in an unusually fine state of preservation disclosed a maximum thickness of 0.57 cm at the origin, which tapered to 62% of that at 60 cm, and which further tapered to 43%, measured 5 cm from the tip. Geibig's series documents maximum fuller widths between 1.8 and 2.25 cm. A number of eleventh century swords with blades corresponding to Oakeshott's types Xa and XI have profiles and inscriptions of a nature most consistent with type 5, except that they have fullers well below 1.8 cm in width. Tapering of the fuller for type 5 may run a gamut anywhere from none to a reduction to 78%, measured at 40 cm from the origin of the blade. Ingelrii inscriptions may be found on blades of this type as are iron inlaid inscriptions incorporating **ME FECIT** and the **IN NOMINE DOMINI** invocation.

[1] Jan Petersen, *De Norske Vikingesverd* (Oslo, 1919). An English translation by Kristin Noer of portions of this work may be found at www.vikingsword.com/petersen.

[2] R.E. Mortimer Wheeler, *London and the Vikings (London Museum Catalogues: No. 1)* (London, 1927), pp. 29–37.

[3] R. Ewart Oakeshott, *The Archaeology of Weapons* (London, 1960), pp. 132–139.

[4] Alfred Geibig, *Beiträge zur morphologischen Entwicklung des Schwertes im Mittelalter: Eine Analyse des Fundmaterials vom ausgehenden 8. bis zum 12. Jahrhundert aus Sammlungen der Bundesrepublik Deutschland* (Neumünster, 1991).

[5] A. N. Kirpichnikov, 'Drevnerusskoye oruzhiye (vyp. I) Mechi i Sabli, IX–XIII vv', *Arkheologiya SSR* (1966), pp. E1–36.

[6] Leena Tomanterä, *Kaksi Köyliön miekkahautaa. Vanhankartanon C-kalmiston haudat XVI ja XVII* (Helsinki, 1978).

[7] Mikael Jakobsson, *Krigarideologi och vikingatida svärdstypologi* (Stockholm, 1992), pp. 24–78, 178–179.

[8] Wheeler (1927), p. 34; Jakobsson (1992), p. 178.

[9] Jakobsson (1992), pp. 63–65, 208–240.

[10] Elis Behmer, *Das Zweischneidige Schwert der Germanischen Völkerwanderungszeit* (Stockholm, 1939) and Wilfried Menghin, *Das Schwert im Frühen Mittelalter* (Stuttgart, 1983).

[11] Michael Müller-Wille, 'Das Prunkschwert aus dem Schatz der Münsterkirche zu Essen und weitere Prunkschwerter aus ottonischer und karolingischer Zeit in Europa', *Das Zeremonialschwert der Essener Domschatzkammer*, ed. Alfred Pothmann (Münster, 1995), p. 140, fig. 3.

[12] Petersen (1919), p. 59.

[13] Geibig (1991), pp. 90–100.

[14] Petersen (1919), pp. 89, 94 and Jakobsson (1992), pp. 209–210.

[15] An example from Neuenburgersee now in the Schweizerischen Landesmuseum in Zurich, accession LM 860, is illustrated and described in Hugo Schneider, *Waffen im Schweizerischen Landesmuseum: Griffwaffen I* (Zurich, 1980), p. 15. See also Jakobsson (1992), pp. 209–210 and 220.

[16] Petersen (1919), p. 90.

[17] Petersen (1919), pp. 64–65.

[18] Petersen (1919), pp. 76–77.

[19] Petersen (1919), pp. 106–111.

[20] Mikael Jakobsson (1992), pp. 210 and 221.

[21] Willem J. H. Willems and Jaap Ypey, 'Ein Angelsächsisches Schwert aus der Maas bei Wessen, Provinz Limburg (Niederlande)', *Archäologisches Korrespondenblatt* 15 (1985), pp. 103–113; H.R. Ellis Davidson, *The Sword in Anglo-Saxon England* (Oxford, 1962), pp. 69–71.

[22] Petersen (1919), pp. 158–167.

[23] Geibig (1991), pp. 143–147, 151.

[24] Petersen (1919), p. 160.

[25] Petersen (1919), pp. 55–58.

[26] Petersen (1919), p. 161.

[27] Geibig (1991), pp. 83–90, 150–154.

Plate I

Examples of pattern-welding. Plate VI from A.L. Lorange, *Den Yngre Jernalders Sværd* (Bergen, 1889), reproduced at 75% of original size. The second sword from the left, Bergens Museum No. 883, has a pattern-welded core made up of three bands with aligned alternating twisted and straight areas in which adjacent bands have an opposite twist.

Plate II

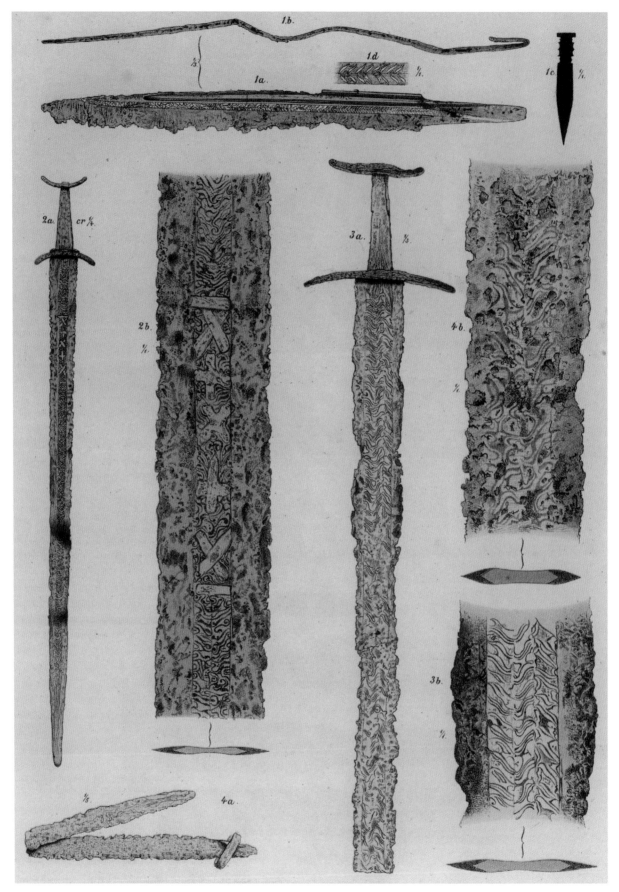

More examples of pattern-welding. Plate V from A.L. Lorange, *Den Yngre Jernalders Sværd* (Bergen, 1889), reduced to 75% of original size. The left sword, Bergens Museum No. 2605, has an iron inlay over a pattern-welded core.

Plate III

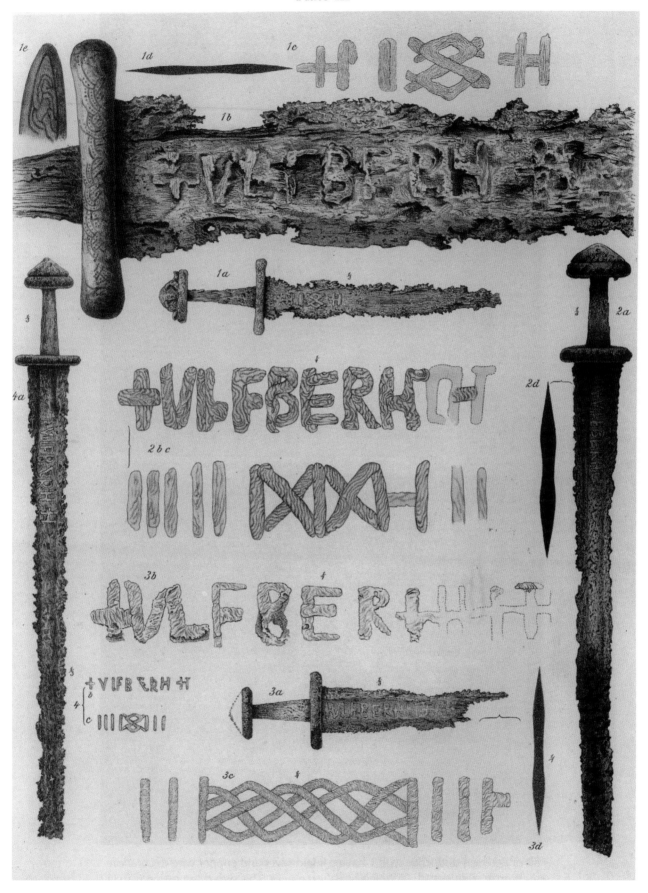

Examples from the collection of Bergens Museum, Norway of **+ULFBERHT+** twisted laminated rod iron inlaid inscriptions and of the corresponding geometric inlays found on the opposite blade face. Plate I from A.L. Lorange, *Den Yngre Jernalders Sværd* (Bergen, 1889), reduced to 75% of original size.

Plate IV

Hilt of Petersen distinctive type 1 having inlaid silver and copper wire decoration and bronze plaques with 'gripping-beast' ornament. This sword, accession C20317 at Oslo, is further illustrated and discussed on pp. 32–33 herein. Photograph by Eirik Irgens Johnsen, courtesy of and copyright by the Universitetets Oldsaksamling.

Plate V

Sword of Petersen type H found in the Maas River near Kessel, Province Noord-Brabant, Holland.
Restored by Jaap Ypey, who notes the presence of a bronze strip on the tang apparently applied as a shim to
fit the upper guard, residual scabbard wood adherent to the blade by the crossguard and patches of residual
leather which once lined the scabbard with the hairy side facing the blade. For further details, see Jaap Ypey,
'Einige wikingerzeitliche Schwerter aus den Niederlanden', *Offa* 41 (1984), pp. 213–225.

Plate VI

A pommel of Petersen Type H with copper and silver wire inlaid onto an iron base. Some strands appear to alternate between silver and copper at a regular interval, indicating a twisted pair of wires. Dimensions: 4.54 cm in the axis of the blade by 8.07 cm in width and 2.96 cm in thickness. Photograph by Doug Whitman.

A cast bronze crossguard of both form and decoration characteristic of Petersen type O. A similar cast upper guard which was an isolated find in Haddebyer Noor, accession 13018 in the Wikinger Museum Haithabu, remains unfinished, retaining flanges from the casting process. Dimensions: 1.53 cm in the axis of the blade by 10.82 cm in width and 1.62 cm in thickness. Photograph by Doug Whitman.

Plate VII

Hilt of Petersen type I with an extensive plating of silver and copper wire and the remains of a leather covered grip. Found in a fishing net in Strandefjorden near Nes, N. Aurdal, Oppland, Norway and recorded as having been a gift from hotel owner Lage Fossheim to Jan Petersen. Accession C23127 in the Universitetets Oldsaksamling. Photograph by Eirik Irgens Johnsen, courtesy of and copyright by the Universitetets Oldsaksamling, negative 23353.

Plate VIII

Hilt of Petersen type T having an overall silver plating with the underlying iron base exposed by the decoration. This sword, accession C18454 in Oslo, is further illustrated and discussed on p. 108 herein. Photograph by Eirik Irgens Johnsen, courtesy of and copyright by the Universitetets Oldsaksamling.

Catalogue of Examples
Ian G. Peirce

Private Collection

Date: fifth or sixth century
Blade length: 71.5 cm
Condition: excellent

We do not know any details related to the finding of this sword which was in the collection of D'Acre Edwards, who died in 1961. His fine collection was initially sent to Gorringes at Lewes, East Sussex, but eventually was auctioned at Christie's in London. It is however significant that a similar pattern-welded sword blade, many spear heads, one of which was pattern-welded, and several early axe heads, including one from the seventh century, were in the collection of D'Acre Edwards.[1]

This fine pattern-welded blade is in an excellent state of preservation. Close inspection of the tang and shoulders of the blade indicated that it was never an overly long blade and probably no more than 28.5 inches in length. Maximum blade width is 5.5 cm. The central fullers are 2.3 to 2.5 cm wide and run almost to the end of the well-preserved tip. The fullers also continue up the broad sturdy tang which is also pattern-welded. Both cutting edges are in excellent condition and bear evidence of much use. Indeed, both cutting edges remain extremely sharp.

It is the sheer beauty of the pattern-welding to which one's eyes are drawn.[2] It appears that the central body of the blade was assembled from twisted bars of three layered material stacks, the two steels being in alternating order. The resulting pattern was achieved by the degree of grinding to which the blade was subjected.[3] By studying both sides of the blade, it becomes clear that the structure patterns run in different directions. This has led the metallographers in Berlin to deduce that the blade is composed of two layers which were then folded over and welded together. The cutting edges were then fabricated separately and later welded to the central body.

Quite remarkably a whole collection of trace elements was found in the blade, namely, Gallium, Yttrium, Hafnium and Thallium with 'significantly elevated contents of Chromium, Yttrium, Niobium, Molybdenum, Hafnium and Thallium found in the cutting edge material'.[4]

There was originally a significant amount of residual scabbard material sticking to one side of the blade, close to the hilt.

[1] David Nicolle, *Medieval Warfare Source Book;* Volume 1: Warfare in Western Christendom (London, 1995), pp. 35 and 82.
[2] See the photographs showing both sides of the blade towards the point. It is indeed awesome to dwell upon the skill of these swordsmiths of some 1,500 years ago. The quality of their raw material would not have been consistent, and yet we can regard with great respect the product of the strength of their arms and the sweat of their brow.
[3] See p. 7 herein.
[4] For a complete scientific appraisal of this important weapon see Christian Segebade's report.

← Full length view showing the robust tang and broad fuller of this pattern-welded sword blade of the Migration Period. Digital composite prepared from a photograph by the Bundesanstalt für Materialforschung und-prüfung, Berlin and a photograph from the archives of Ewart Oakeshott.

→ Photographs prepared at the Bundesanstalt für Materialforschung und-prüfung, Berlinprüfung of the pattern-welding of this blade.

27

National Museum of Ireland, Dublin
WK-25

Date: eighth century
Find-place: near Askeaton, County Limerick, Ireland
Overall length: 90.0 cm *Blade length:* 74.5 cm
Length of cross: 11.2 cm *Length of grip:* 9.4 cm
Balance point: 16.6 cm
Condition: excellent condition in all respects

According to Wakeman, this weapon was found in a river near Askeaton, County Limerick, about the year 1848. Presented by the Rev. Robert J. Gabbett, late of Foynes, to W.F. Wakeman and by him to the Collection of the Royal Irish Academy.

The finely tapering blade of this important sword appears to have received no hazardous forms of cleaning and remains in an unusually excellent condition with only a few small areas of light pitting. The fullers are shallow and as Bøe recorded, indistinct, and they run to almost the whole length of the blade.[1] One area close to the hilt has some deep corrosion, but this allows us a glimpse of the structure of the blade metal, which appears to be composed of bundles of rods arranged longitudinally, across the whole width of the blade.

The canoe-shaped cross is long, slender, and elegant and bears no traces of any former decoration. The lower element of the pommel is a smaller version of the cross and is firmly attached to the long, low and comparatively thin upper portion. The latter is divided into three parts by two sets of parallel grooves, one set of which still retains its hammered-in strands of silver wire. This thin upper portion sits on a raised 'lip' which skirts its boundary. There has been some attempt to decorate this lip by applying two vertical and parallel cuts every 1.5 cm or so around its length.[2] The hefty tang carries two iron mountings with turned-up ends like the cross. These are serrated on the outer edges and recessed to accommodate and locate the grip.

Jan Petersen makes many interesting comments upon this type. When his book was published, in 1919, he knew of eight examples, one of which had a single-edged blade.[3] For four of these, only the hilts were recovered from the graves. The curved upper guard and cross of this specimen are not typical of a type A, but after careful consideration, no other came even close to fitting the equation. Within Petersen's other categories it may be seen that many subtle variations existed. None of these with blades were pattern-welded or bore inscriptions. He also stated that this type had the narrowest and among the smallest of blades from the Viking Age. Distribution is wide across Norway, but it must be remembered that the sample is very small. Behmer placed this in his type VIII.[4]

[1] Johs. Bøe, 'Norse Antiquities in Ireland', *Viking Antiquities in Great Britain and Ireland, Part III*, ed. Haakon Shetelig (Oslo, 1940), p. 83 and fig. 53b.
[2] See H.R. Ellis Davidson, *The Sword in Anglo-Saxon England* (Oxford, 1962), pp. 54–55 and fig. 82. The 'slightly upturned ends are not rivets'.
[3] Petersen was clearly unaware of the Askeaton sword, found in 1848, commenting that he did not know of this type outside of Norway.
[4] For another example with similar ears on the pommel and curved guards see Elis Behmer, *Das Zweischneidige Schwert der Germanischen Völkerwanderungszeit* (Stockholm, 1939), fig. LXI, 1a and 1b, Statens Historika Museum, Stockholm, accession 2194.

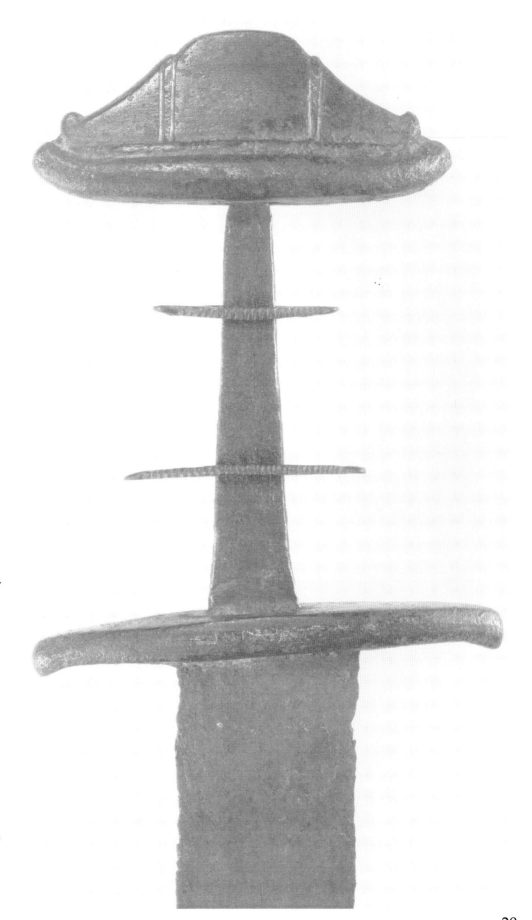

← Full length view of WK-25. Photograph courtesy of and copyright by the National Museum of Ireland.

→ Hilt of WK-25. The two loose devices about the tang are described by Bøe as 'iron mountings, bent like the crossbars, and grooved along the edges' and are shown one against the upper guard and the other against the cross in fig. 53 of Bøe. Photograph courtesy of and copyright by the National Museum of Ireland.

Date: eighth century
Find-place: Bildsø, Denmark
Overall length: 59.4 cm   *Blade length:* 41.3 cm (incomplete)
Length of cross: 10.6 cm   *Length of grip:* 10.1 cm (a weld is noted)
Condition: the hilt remains in an excellent condition; the blade has been electrolytically cleaned, but the process has revealed with some clarity its structure

The entry in the museum records for this stunningly hilted weapon is under the year 1877 and states 'Found in Bildsø; present from a royal gamekeeper's wife. Sword and scabbard fitting (chape)'.[1]

The fragmentary blade appears to have been either electrolytically cleaned or subjected to caustic cleaning and most callously, but this action has revealed two bands of pattern-welding. These are predominantly of chevron formation, entirely so on the side illustrated, with *rosendamast* being present in about equal proportions with *streifendamast* upon the other. Each of the pattern-welded bands is about 0.9 cm wide.[2] One can also easily view the structure of the cutting edges which had been each welded to the central blade section.

All elements of the hilt surfaces are constructed of sheet silver and the damage to the pommel allows the thickness of the precious metal to be determined as slightly less than 0.1 cm. There are also traces of gilding on all elements of the hilt. The decorative pommel is most exquisitely fashioned and must originally have been formed on some inner core of wood or other organic material which provided an inner supporting structure. On the better preserved side of the pommel, the side shown in the illustration, are a central and two flanking panels of decoration, in relief and which appear to represent tiny beasts gripping one another. Only the central panel, with similar decoration, remains on the reverse side. Rivet heads are seen at the extremities of the upper guard on the surface facing the grip, but as these are hollow, they clearly have a decorative function only. Two copper tabs protrude alongside each rivet head; they are pierced with a tiny hole and probably in some way had the structural function of holding or tying the upper guard and pommel rigidly together. The crossguard, also of silver, bears no ornamentation and again has false rivets at its extremities. It is not damaged and therefore it is not possible to determine the material of which the core is constructed.

The scabbard, which has lost its lower end, appears to be decorated in a similar fashion to the sword's pommel, i.e. a series of contorted fighting beasts.

[1] No details of the context of the find are given. It was first published in *Mémoires de la société royale des Antiquaires du Nord 1872–1877 (Séances de la société 1877)*, p. 385. A similar example to this has been found in Germany, to which some scholars have assigned a very early date, c. 800.
[2] For a variety of configurations of pattern-welding see especially Jorma Leppäaho, *Späteisenzeitliche Waffen aus Finnland: Schwertinschriften und Waffenverzierungen des 9.–12. Jahrhunderts* (Helsinki, 1964), pp. 31–32.

↖ Copenhagen C3118 full length view. Photograph courtesy of and copyright the National Museum of Denmark.

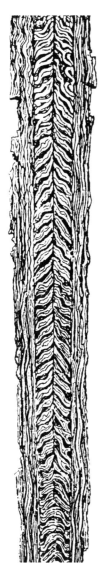

↑ Detail of pattern-welded
blade from drawing of C3118
in *Mémoires de la société
royale des Antiquaires du
Nord 1872–1877 (Séances
de la société 1877)*, p. 385.

↗ Drawing of scabbard
chape associated with
C3118, from 1877 as above.

→ Copenhagen C3118 detail
of hilt. Photograph courtesy
of and copyright the National
Museum of Denmark. See
also Elis Behmer, *Das
Zweischneidige Schwert der
Germanischen
Völkerwanderungszeit*
(Stockholm, 1939), fig. LIII, 2
for another photo of this hilt.

C20317

Date: eighth century
Find-place: Steinvik farm, Hol Lødingen parish, Nordland, Norway
Overall length: 100.1 cm *Blade length:* 83.8 cm
Length of cross: 8.3 cm *Length of grip:* 10.1 cm
Condition: hilt in excellent condition; blade much corroded

This handsome eighth century sword was found in a grave at a farm called Steinvik, in the parish of Hol Lødingen, Nordland. It was discovered close to a small mound of sand, the skeleton lying with its head to the east with the sword on the left side. Among the other artifacts, all of which were on the right side of the skeleton, were an axe, pieces of a shield boss, a domestic axe, a hammer, scissors, a knife and a file. A spearhead was lying some 2 meters away. The skull had a 4 to 5 cm long cut on the forehead, but this was not the cause of death, for the cut had healed.

This is a beautifully proportioned and long blade. It has shallow fullers and the cutting edges, although corroded, still have good definition. Originally it was some 6 cm wide at the cross and is pattern-welded.

The hilt is most richly decorated.[1] Each side of the boat-shaped cross is adorned with three beautifully wrought, tiny rectangular bronze plaques, each of which contain minute animal ornamentation with all other areas of the lateral faces filled in with strips of silver wire, hammered onto the surface.[2] The upper and lower surfaces of the cross, towards the grip and blade, are presently without signs of embellishment. The upper guard is the same shape and size as the cross and is decorated in an identical manner. It also retains good quantities of the applied silver strip. It is separated from the trilobated pommel by a band of closely twisted silver wire, much of which remains. The large central lobe is isolated from the two smaller outer ones by two sets of twisted silver wires.[3] Embedded within it is an almost rectangular bronze plaque, inside which is another group of tiny, writhing animals. Flattened strips of twisted silver and copper wire with an alternating chevron pattern highlight the inset panels and pommel lobulation. Otherwise, all other areas are covered with hammered on strands of silver strip.[4] The reverse side of the upper portion of the hilt is identical to that just described. The upper guard and pommel were held together by rivets, one of which remains. Each one of the animal plaques is different and it is not possible to identify any species.

The quality of the decoration of this outstanding example makes it quite clearly the weapon of an important chieftain.

[1] See Jan Petersen, *De Norske Vikingesverd* (Oslo, 1919), fig. 56 and p. 65. This sword is also discussed and illustrated in James Graham-Campbell, *Viking Artefacts: A Select Catalogue* (London, 1980), pp. 69–70 and p. 243 and in Michael Müller-Wille, 'Das Prunkschwert aus dem Schatz der Münsterkirche zu Essen und weitere Prunkschwerter aus ottonischer und karolingischer Zeit in Europa', *Das Zeremonialschwert der Essener Domschatzkammer*, ed. Alfred Pothmann (Münster, 1995), pp. 135, 148 (transposed illustration) and 149 (caption).
[2] The silver wire is appropriately 0.1 cm thick.
[3] Each set contains two wires.
[4] Though here and there a strand of copper has been used, perhaps as a result of a repair.

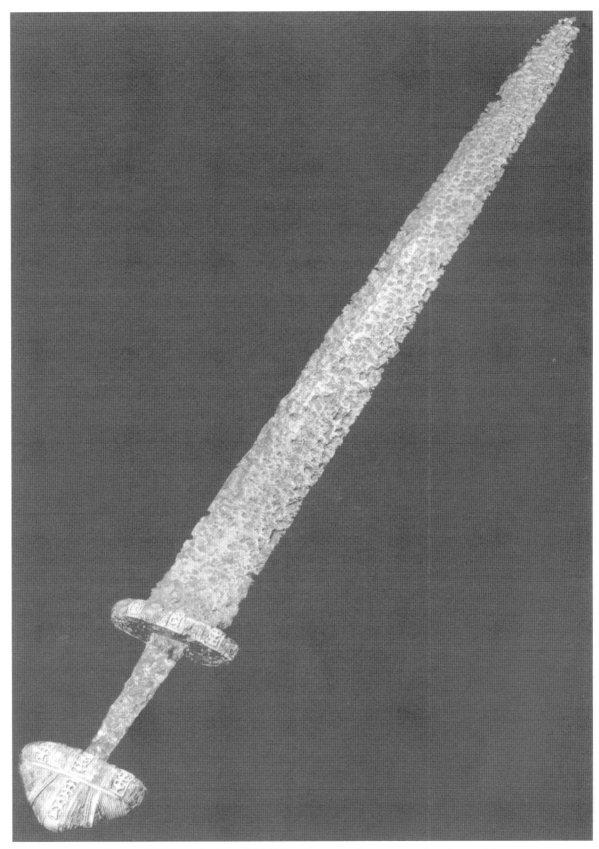

A diagonal full length view of C20317. Photograph courtesy of and copyright
by the Universitetets Oldsaksamling; negative 11506. A colour view of the hilt
is reproduced herein as plate IV.

Date: late eighth to early ninth century
Find-place: between Horn and Roermond, Province Limburg, Holland
Overall length: 101.8 cm *Blade length:* 84.8 cm
Length of cross: 7.7 cm *Length of grip:* 10.5 cm
Balance point: 20.3 cm
Condition: excavated

Found in 1971 between Horn and Roermond, in the Limburg Province of the Netherlands, by V. D. Zwaag, during a dredging operation.

The blade of this well-tapered large weapon is in excavated condition but fortunately some areas of the original surface have survived, especially on both sides near to the crossguard. The broad shallow fullers run to a point of some 10.5 cm from the well-preserved tip and even although areas of organic material are in evidence they are both easily discernible (width close to cross 1.9 cm). Jan Petersen knew of 22 specimens of type B from Norway of which 14 were double-edged and 8 single edged. Of these one was pattern-welded and another possibly so, otherwise they were all without pattern-welding or inscriptions (inlaid decoration).[1]

The sword under consideration is therefore of huge importance for not only is it pattern-welded, but it also has iron-inlaid devices set into its blade.

Centred some 9 cm from the crossguard on one side of the blade is a circular swirl of pattern-welding reminiscent of some of those illustrated by Leppäaho.[2] This is followed by a straight bar across the whole width of the fuller and yet another, a further 3 cm toward the point. Both of these are joined by a central bar.

Further evidence of pattern-welding activity is discernible on both sides of the blade.

The crossguard has survived remarkably well, with much of the original surface still intact. Each lateral face has been bevelled to form a low central ridge.[3] The stub ends of the crossguard also bear decoration. On each end three grooves had been cut (in line with the blade) into which decorative strips of copper alloy had been forced. Two strips on each end still survive.[4]

The hefty tang tapers in both width and thickness towards the pommel and is still covered by a considerable amount of wooden grip material.

The upper guard is heavily corroded but sufficient remains to state with certainty that it was a smaller version of the crossguard. One small area sports its original surface. One end has a central groove (in line with the blade) which would almost certainly have contained a copper-alloy strip.

The pommel is much corroded and was riveted to the upper guard with the two components separated by a thin silver alloy sheet which survives.[5]

[1] Jan Petersen, *De Norske Vikingesverd* (Oslo, 1919), p. 61.
[2] Jorma Leppäaho, *Späteisenzeitliche Waffen aus Finnland: Schwertinschriften und Waffenverzierungen des 9.–12. Jahrhunderts* (Helsinki, 1964), pl. 10, 2c.
[3] Ibid., fig. 53.
[4] This is the first time I have seen crossguard ends decorated in this way.
[5] Petersen states that none of the 22 he inspected had the pommel riveted to the upper guard.

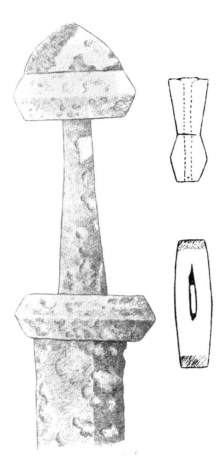

↑ Figure 53 from Petersen (1919), p. 62, of C16001 in the Universitetets Oldsaksamling, Oslo; the typical Petersen type B. Captioned Jarstad, V. Slidre, Krist. 1/2.

→ Detail of the hilt and the side of the pattern-welded blade having iron-inlaid devices. While the overall dimensions and profile of this hilt most closely resemble Petersen's type B, the presence of rivets securing the pommel to the upper guard and the presence of a small amount of applied nonferrous decoration would argue instead for an early type H as, for type B, Petersen, p. 61, states, in Kristin Noer's translation at www.vikingsword.com/petersen/ptsn061b.html (8 Feb. 1998), 'Guards and pommel are without metal covering or other ornamentation. The pommel … was never attached to the upper guard with rivets.' Photograph by Doug Whitman.

← Full length view of the sword dredged from the Maas floodplain between Roermond and Horn. Photograph by Doug Whitman.

↓ Idealized scale diagram of the copper alloy decoration present on each end of the iron crossguard.

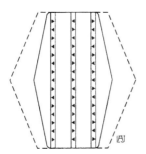

Date: ninth century
Find-place: Vig farm, Flaa Sogn parish, Naesby, Hallingdalen, Norway
Overall length: 102.4 cm *Blade length:* 86 cm
Length of cross: 8.5 cm *Length of grip:* 8.5 cm
Balance point: 20 cm
Condition: very good and boasting some areas of original surface

This double-edged ninth century specimen was found by ploughing just below the earth's surface, on the hillside of a farm called Vig in the parish of Flaa Sogn, Naesby in Hallingdalen.

The massive 86 cm blade is very similar to C11014 (pp. 72–73) and tapers gently to a spatulate tip. The fullers are nicely defined and taper to fade some 12 cm from the point. There is a slight bend in the blade and, as one would expect, it corresponds with a point of bad corrosion. This example does not appear to be pattern-welded. Both cutting edges are nicely formed and in some foci, boast their original surfaces.

The short chunky cross, typical of this type, is boat-shaped in section but with blunt ends. It remains in an excellent state of preservation, considering its burial in the ground. It is bevelled in two directions, both on its lateral faces and ends. The massive, sturdy tang is terminated by a huge flat, triangular pommel, the top and bottom parts being separated by two deep parallel, thin cuts 3 mm. apart.[1] The top triangular portion has further similar incised decoration, which is simple but effective. As with the blade, some areas of the hilt still sport their original surfaces.[2] The pommel tilts to one side and this possibly may have resulted from its having received a blow from, for example, a plough, especially as the museum register states quite clearly that it was found 'just below the earth's surface'.

To conclude, it is extremely rare to find a Viking Age sword with an overall length of more than 1 metre. Even considering the huge pommel, this weapon has a very poor balance, and consequently does not handle easily.[3] Petersen lists this hilt type as having a wide distribution.[4] This type is among the heaviest of sword types and Jan Petersen determined the weight of C777 as a massive 1.896 kg (4.17 lb).

---

[1] See Jan Petersen, *De Norske Vikingesverd* (Oslo, 1919), fig. 58.
[2] It may well be that this weapon had been subject to extreme heat and is therefore exhibiting *glødeskall. Glødeskall* refers to a compound of iron and oxygen (Fe_3O_4) created when an iron object is subjected to intense heat. *Glødeskall* forms a shell (*skal*) or skin around the object and, as long as it is intact, provides some protection against corrosion. However, it often has minute cracks, which may permit corrosion to quickly attack the object behind the shell.
[3] Lee Jones and I both handled this weapon in 1993 and determined its point of balance at that time.
[4] Petersen, pp. 67–68. See also C24217, pp. 40–41 herein, the sword from North Arhus, Hjartdal, Telemark.

→ Detail of hilt. Photograph courtesy of
and copyright Universitetets
Oldsaksamling, negative 23352/16.

← Full length view of C777. Photograph
by Ove Holst, courtesy of and copyright
Universitetets Oldsaksamling, negative
21581/34.

British Museum, London

1873, 12-19 233

Date: ninth to tenth century
Find-place: burial mound at Hov, Hoff, Aker, Oslo, Norway
Overall length: 95.6 cm *Blade length:* 78.6 cm
Length of cross: 8.7 cm *Length of grip:* 9.5 cm
Balance point: 15.9 cm
Condition: generally the blade and the hilt are in a very good excavated condition

According to the museum register, the find spot was 'Norway, Oslo, Aker, Hoff, Hov, burial mound'. It was purchased from Mrs. Frances Elizabeth Thurnam and collected by Dr. John Thurnam.

This is a very broad bladed weapon with a width of 6.2 cm (nearly 2.5 inches) where the blade meets the crossguard. It may have been broken at some stage about 18.5 cm from the point and welded. The fullers are fairly distinct in some places and are 2.5 cm wide at the hilt, after which they taper down and eventually end some 9 cm from the point. Again, the cutting edges are in excellent condition in places. On one side and close to the cross is a coating of organic material sticking to the surface and this is likely to be the remains of a wooden scabbard. Further down the blade there is an area which exhibits the original surface and there is no doubt we have another good example of *glødeskall*. The museum register also states that there is an iron 'inlaid maker's mark of three groups of pattern-welded bars separated by two zones of lattice'. On inspection I could not see this and I could find no mention in the splendid paper on the radiographic study of the swords in the British Museum.[1] However, because I could not see it does not mean it is not there.

The cross is boat-shaped and similar to that shown above in Petersen and two little shallow fullers have been ground out on either side of the lateral faces. The sturdy tang is still firmly embedded in the chunky pommel. Both lateral faces of the pommel each have a single shallow fuller and each appear to have been bounded by two pairs of parallel cuts.

Petersen states that in Norway he was aware of 110 specimens of type C, which is clearly a direct development from type B.[2] Of these, forty were double-edged, like the sword presently under consideration, sixty-seven were single-edged and in three cases it could not be determined.

[1] Janet Lang and Barry Ager, 'Swords of the Anglo-Saxon and Viking Periods in the British Museum: a Radiographic Study', *Weapons and Warfare in Anglo-Saxon England*, ed. Sonia Chadwick Hawkes (Oxford, 1989), pp. 85–122.
[2] Jan Petersen, *De Norske Vikingesverd* (Oslo, 1919) , pp. 66–70. Kristin Noer's English translation of this section of Peterson's text dealing with type C may be found at the Medieval Sword Resource Site, www.vikingsword.com/petersen/ptsn066c.html (20 May 2000).

← Full length view of 1873, 12-19 233. Photograph courtesy of and copyright British Museum.

National Museum of Ireland, Dublin
WK-31

Date: ninth to early tenth century
Find-place: Kilmainham, Dublin, Ireland
Overall length: 82.0 cm *Blade length:* 66.5 cm
Length of cross: 9.0 cm *Length of grip:* 8.0 cm
Condition: complete, but badly corroded overall and with much adherent organic material upon the blade

This is one of many single-edged weapons from the Kilmainham–Island Bridge area. It is included here because it is a complete weapon and in order to draw a comparison between those found in Dublin, of which this is typical, and the two examples in the National Museum, Copenhagen.[1]

The blade is unusually broad with a maximum width at the cross of 7.0 cm.[2] Compared with the two Danish type H examples, the pommel, which is forged in one piece, is extremely angular.

The hilt and the blade do not show any indication of any form of decoration.

The weapon, when handled, feels most unwieldy, owing much to the massive width of the blade, the edges of which are almost parallel all the way to the point.

Wakeman, who seems to have the last word on almost everything, states that this 'broad bladed single-edged sword of iron, with straight cross bar and conical pommel, was found near Kilmainham in the cutting of the great southern and western Railway. Presented by the Governors of Kilmainham, Hospital and the Director of the Railway.'

Plunket painted an excellent watercolour of this important weapon (among others) in 1847.[3]

These single-edged weapons were very common in the ninth and early tenth century alongside other types and they appear to have been much neglected by students of the sword.[4]

[1] Specifically, museum accessions C24550 and C24554 in the National Museum of Denmark which do have different hilt types than this sword.
[2] Johs. Bøe, 'Norse Antiquities in Ireland', *Viking Antiquities in Great Britain and Ireland, Part III*, ed. Haakon Shetelig (Oslo, 1940), p. 12.
[3] See The National Museum of Ireland, *Dublin 1000* (Dublin, 1988), p. 10. This is a splendid booklet which explains discoveries and excavations in Dublin from 1842 to 1981.
[4] It is indeed most rare to see an illustration or indeed a mention of this important class of weapons.

→ Full length view of WK-31. Photograph courtesy of and copyright National Museum of Ireland.

Date: ninth to early tenth century
Find-place: North Arhus farm, Hjartdal parish, Telemark, Norway
Overall length: 92.0 cm *Blade length:* 76 cm
Length of cross: 8.3 cm *Length of grip:* 9.4 cm
Condition: excellent condition due to *glødeskall*

This outstanding weapon possibly came from two or more graves, the contents of which had been mixed together.[1] It was probably discovered in 1909 on North Arhus farm, in the parish of Hjartdal, county of Telemark. While fieldwork was in progress, artifacts were unearthed both above and lower down upon a hill from 'the remains of a mound (cairn) of stones'.[2] It was never possible to determine which things went together or the total number of graves, but other artifacts recovered included two axes, four arrows (probably just the heads), one knife, part of a horse bit, two sickles, and weaving fitments.

The finely tapered blade (5 cm wide at the cross and 4 cm before the curvature of the point) is in almost pristine condition for most of its length and exhibits its wondrous pattern-welding in the manner it must have looked in the ninth (or early tenth) century. The pattern-welding of the main body of the blade focally runs into a good solid cutting edge; however, the cutting edge itself does not appear to be pattern-welded, but to consist of bundles of thin longitudinal rods. The main body of the blade has been cunningly fullered, to reduce the blade weight and improve wieldability.[3] The pattern-welding is exquisite and some of the finest (probably the very best) from the period.[4] It is of the *blodiða* configuration; much like the swirling eddies at the bend of a small stream. Towards the end of the blade the surface corrosion has revealed the structure of the blade in a quite remarkable fashion and in such a manner as to benefit the student of the sword.

The cross is boat-like in shape, unusually small and delicate for a single-edged weapon, and pierced by a broad, acutely tapering tang. Apart from a small lateral crack, it is in excellent condition as indeed is the well-formed, slightly pitted pommel. The hilt is very similar to that shown by Petersen, which was found at Alstad, O. Slidre, Kristian.[5]

Jan Petersen states that this sword type is among the heaviest of all the swords from the Viking Age. As of the publication of his book in 1919, he knew of 110 specimens, 40 with double-edged blades, 67 single-edged and 3 which could not be determined. Furthermore, this type C had a wide distribution over the country and none of those documented by Petersen had a pattern-welded blade.[6]

[1] This most usually occurs when he who discovers the find undertakes the excavation himself.
[2] The artifacts unearthed were found next to a layer of earthen coal.
[3] An unusual feature and one I cannot recall seeing so well preserved on a single-edged blade before. In all probability, this may well be an almost standard feature, but so many of the early single-edged blades are in such poor condition, it is not easy to identify fullers.
[4] See Ewart Oakeshott, *The Archaeology of Weapons* (London, 1960), p. 151.
[5] Jan Petersen, *De Norske Vikingesverd* (Oslo, 1919), p. 66, and fig. 57.
[6] See Petersen, p. 67. Kristin Noer's English translation of this section of Peterson's text dealing with type C, pp. 66–70, may be found at www.vikingsword.com/petersen/ptsn066c.html (20 May 2000).

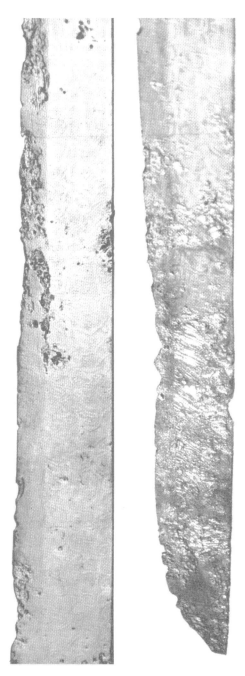

↑ Photographs showing the pattern-welded structure of this single-edged sword blade. The photograph on the left shows two bands, each exhibiting a prominently curved pattern, consistent with the exposed centre of a laminated twisted rod; see diagram on p. 147. The view on the right shows a similar pattern at top, but heavier corrosion has revealed the more linear pattern expected from the periphery of the rod towards the tip of the blade. Photographs by Ian Peirce.

→ Hilt and forte of the blade of C24217. Note the horizontal ridge on the crossguard. Photograph courtesy of and copyright Universitetets Oldsaksamling, negative 24217a.

← Full length view of C24217. Photograph courtesy of and copyright Universitetets Oldsaksamling, negative 24217a.

WK-33

Date: ninth century
Overall length: 92.0 cm *Blade length:* 73 cm
Length of cross: 11.0 cm *Length of grip:* 9.2 cm
Condition: blade heavily corroded, hilt excellent

There is some doubt as to the find-place of this ninth century weapon. Wakeman states that it was 'found in the ancient cemetery at Kilmainham, commonly styled Bully's Acre'. Raghnall Ó Floinn states 'Kilmainham - Islandbridge, Dublin,' where I am certain it was found.[1]

The blade of this regally hilted sword, which is missing its tip, is heavily corroded but still retains some vestiges of the fullers.

Both the crossguard and pommel are constructed of intricate castings of gilt-copper alloy formed upon a core of iron. The decoration on both is identical and consists of vertical, upon the top element of the pommel, and horizontal, upon the lower element of the pommel and the cross, rows of geometric shapes cast in chip-carved technique.[3] The gilt copper matrix is pierced to take these geometric shapes consisting individually of a cluster of three silver rings with a silver centre (ring and dot devices) all set in niello. The effect is stunning and nearly all of these almost identical tiny devices are intact. The two rows around the perimeter (lateral faces) of the cross are separated by two sets of copper and silver wire twisted together and embedded in niello.[4] It must be noted

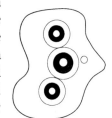

that it is most unusual to find copper and silver wires, twisted together for decorative purposes at so early a date in Ireland. Silver and copper twisted wire also separates the two rows of decoration on the lower portion of the pommel. The upper part is made up of four lobes. The two outer are separated from the two inner by thick twisted silver wire set between two beaded wires on the outside and one beaded wire on the inside. A single beaded silver wire separates the two smaller, central lobes. The lower face of the pommel and upper face of the cross each have the remains of the circle and dot decoration described above. The grip is provided with a scalloped mount made of brass and decorated with stylized plant motifs.[5]

The sheer quality of the decoration upon the hilt of this prestige weapon indicates the length to which contemporary artisans would go to entice their customers. This hilt is truly a great work of art.

It is of a type also found at Ophus Vang, Hedemarken Ved Moss, Smaalenene, the Island of Eigg and other examples [only the hilts] from later datable contexts in Finland.[2]

Jan Petersen lists eleven type D hilts found in Norway, two of which are without blades, and nine of which are of the double-edged blade variety, of which one is pattern-welded. As a type, they are among the heaviest swords of the Viking Age. C8095, for example, has a weight of 1.476 kg (3.25 lb).

← Full length view of WK-33. Photograph courtesy of and copyright National Museum of Ireland.

→ Hilt of WK-33. Petersen interpreted the repeating elements on these ferrules or *véttrim* as animal heads.[6] Photograph courtesy of and copyright National Museum of Ireland.

↙ Diagram of one of the repeating elements from the upper guard. Copper alloy is shown as light gray, silver as white and niello as dark gray.

[1] *From Viking to Crusader: The Scandinavians and Europe 800 to 1200* (22nd Council of Europe Exhibition) (Copenhagen, 1992), p. 292 , cat. no. 243. See also Johs. Bøe, 'Norse Antiquities in Ireland', *Viking Antiquities in Great Britain and Ireland, Part III*, ed. Haakon Shetelig (Oslo, 1940), pp. 21–22 and George Coffey and E.C.R. Armstrong, 'Scandinavian Objects Found at Island-Bridge and Kilmainham', *Proceedings of the Royal Irish Academy* vol. XXVIII, sect. C (1910), p. 113 and plate IV, no. 3. Also H.R. Ellis Davidson, Plate IV b. Raghnall Ó Floinn draws attention to the fact that this is the most elaborate of the 40 plus swords from the Kilmainham-Island-Bridge cemetery.
[2] See footnotes 1, 2, and 3 for sword C1572 from Copenhagen on p. 44. See also Coffey and Armstrong, handle of a sword found at Island-Bridge, (museum No. 1906:467). Sir William Wilde's No. 2361, p. 112 and fig. 2. Also Bøe, p. 22 and fig. 6. Note the similarity in design to the sword under examination.
[3] As stated in footnote 1 above.
[4] The contrast of the blackness of the niello and the alternating redness of copper and brightness of the silver is strikingly beautiful.
[5] See Jan Petersen, *De Norske Vikingesverd* (Oslo, 1919), fig. 82.
[6] Ibid., p. 70.

C1572

Date: ninth century
Find-place: Bjørnsholm; Søndersø; N. Jutland, Denmark
Overall length: 90.3 cm *Blade length:* 73.5 cm
Length of cross: 10.4 cm *Length of grip:* 9.1 cm
Condition: excavated condition; hilt excellent, blade corroded and in three pieces

This prestige weapon was found in 1883, by a retired farmer, in the lake of Søndersø, apparently with a thigh bone along side it. Others of this type have been found at Ophus, Vang, Hedemarken;[1] Ved Moss, Smaalenene;[2] the Island of Eigg[3] and the Kilmainham site in Dublin,[4] with other examples represented only by the hilts from later datable contexts in Finland. These, excluding those from Helsinki, may well have emanated from the same or closely associated workshops, so similar are the ideas and schemes behind the overall design and geometric patterns upon the hilts.

The blade is pattern-welded, broken, or corroded through, in two places. The pattern-welding is of two bands, in a herringbone or chevron configuration, with the tips facing the hilt. Each band is 1.0 cm wide. Heavy corrosion and the remains of scabbard fragments adhering to the blade surface tend to cloud the issue but one smooth black, better preserved area clearly indicates a very shallow fuller, 2 cm wide and corresponding to the width of the pattern-welding.

The core of the hilt is of iron, onto which has been applied, in deep relief, a layer of bronze or brass diamond shaped stellate devices surrounded by silver wire strips parallel to the length of the blade upon the guards and pommel, but perpendicular to the blade upon the similarly decorated metallic grip. The hilt still retains more than ninety percent of its original decorative covering. The starlike strips are continuous, passing entirely around the grip, and both ends of the latter, are terminated by another continuous strip of stylized 'bug-eye monster' heads.[5] The grip face of the upper guard carries intersecting and parallel bronze inlaid lines, forming a pattern of repeating diamonds. The decoration, which was certainly similar, has not survived on the grip and blade faces of the crossguard.

Such is the decorative quality of this type of sword, that it would be all too easy to relegate them to the status of purely ceremonial weapons, but let us be in no doubt, here we are dealing with true weapons of war. In essence we have one of the most strikingly beautiful sword hilts one could ever wish to encounter.

[1] Jan Petersen, *De Norske Vikingesverd* (Oslo, 1919), p. 72.
[2] Ibid., p. 73.
[3] See J. Anderson, *Scotland in Pagan Times*, p. 49, fig. 36 and *Proceedings of the Society of Antiquaries of Scotland*, vol. 12, pl. XXX. See also M. Davis, 'Conservation and Analysis of the Eigg Sword Hilt', *Metal 95, Proceedings of the International Conference of Metals Conservators*, pp. 183–189.
[4] Johs. Bøe, 'Norse Antiquities in Ireland', *Viking Antiquities in Great Britain and Ireland, Part III*, ed. Haakon Shetelig (Oslo, 1940), pp. 21–22 and fig. 5.
[5] See especially George Coffey and E.C.R. Armstrong, 'Scandinavian Objects Found at Island-Bridge and Kilmainham', *Proceedings of the Royal Irish Academy* vol. XXVIII, sect. C (1910), pp. 107–122 and pl. IV. Also *From Viking to Crusader: The Scandinavians and Europe 800 to 1200* (22nd Council of Europe Exhibition) (Copenhagen, 1992), cat. no. 243 by Raghnall ÓFloinn and cat. no. 109 by Henriette Lyngstrøm and Else Roesdahl. See also the final paragraph of WK-33, the sword from the National Museum of Ireland, on p. 42.

← Copenhagen C1572 full length view. Photograph courtesy of and copyright by the National Museum of Denmark, negative 16259.

→ Copenhagen C1572 detail of hilt fragment. Photograph courtesy of and copyright by the National Museum of Denmark, negative 10422.

A colour photograph of this hilt may be found in *The Vikings in England and in their Danish Homeland* (London, 1981), p. 45 with description on p. 65, cat. no. D12-2.

Petersen distinctive type 2

Særtype 2 features wide, ridged guards and has a trilobed pommel in which the centre lobe is taller than those on the side.

As with distinctive type 1, Petersen regarded this type as a degenerative simplification of older Migration Period hilts which had a pommel with a tall middle section flanked on either side by a stylized animal head, such as may be seen in Behmer's types V and VIII.

← Fig. 72, cropped below, from Jan Petersen, *De Norske Vikingesverd* (Oslo, 1919), pp. 85–86. This reference example, C12009 from Rimstad, Hedrum, J.L., is noted by Petersen to have been decorated with silver plates which were secured by having been hammered into grooves inscribed upon the pommel and guards. The pommel of this example is secured directly to the tang and pattern-welded inlays are present in the blade.

Petersen type E

Most characteristic of this type is a fairly massive iron hilt decorated with an array of relatively closely spaced circular or oval indentations upon the faces of the pommel and guards, which frequently may also be decorated with parallel inlaid silver or bronze strips. Inlays set just back from the edge may accentuate the boundaries of the faces of the hilt components and the furrows between the pommel lobes. Pommels are usually three lobed and have a profile similar to that seen in type D and in distinctive types 1 and 2, though in some instances there can be loss of the lobation and a more semicircular profile.

The majority of examples have a double-edged blade, but in Petersen's series, just under twenty percent had single-edged blades. Petersen regarded this as an early type, with origins at least as early as the first half of the ninth century, and notes that the type seems particularly associated with the region around Trondheim, Norway.

Jan Petersen, *De Norske Vikingesverd* (Oslo, 1919), pp. 75–80.

→ Pl. I, fig. 1, B6748a, from Jan Petersen, *De Norske Vikingesverd* (Oslo, 1919), captioned Hjelle, Forde. N.B., two thirds actual size.

Petersen type F

This is a simple type with plain iron guards and a characteristically small and knob like pommel, also of unadorned iron. The pommel usually has a rectangular cross section and may be either rounded in contour or faceted with sharply defined edges. The guards typically have an oval cross section with blunted ends, although in some examples the faces of the guards meet more acutely to form somewhat pointed ends.

The majority of the examples in Petersen's series had single-edged blades and he noticed neither pattern-welding or inlaid inscriptions in any of the blades associated with type F hilts. Petersen considered this type to be associated with the first half of the ninth century and suggests that it possibly represents a continuation of the tradition of one of those Migration Period types having small pommels or, conversely, that it may represent a simplification from the contemporary type G.

← Fig. 67, C6409, from Jan Petersen, *De Norske Vikingesverd* (Oslo, 1919), pp. 80–84, captioned Habberstad, Eidsvold, Akh., one half actual size.

Fig. 67. Habberstad, Eidsvold, Akh. ½.

Petersen type G

The defining characteristic of the uncommon type G is the scrolled upper guard, which is spiralled away from the grip. This scrolling is usually, but not always, reflected in the crossguard. The pommel is small, knob like and usually with a rectangular cross section, exactly as is seen with type F. The *guards and pommel are of plain unadorned iron.*

In Petersen's limited series, the majority of these hilts are mounted upon single-edged blades. He considered the type to be contemporary with or to slightly predate type F and speculates on the possibility that type F could represent a simplification of type G in which the scrolling of the guards has been abandoned. Considering the similarities of the two types in form and their preferential distribution in eastern Norway, a relationship between the two types seems obvious, however, it seems equally plausible that type G could represent an elaboration of type F.

→ Fig. 71, C1554, from Jan Petersen, *De Norske Vikingesverd* (Oslo, 1919), pp. 84–85, captioned Dale, Ø. Slidre, Krist.

Fig. 71. Dale, O. Slidre, Krist.

Date: late ninth century
Find-place: Tude River, in the old ford between Heinng and Naesby, Denmark
Overall length: 94.7 cm *Blade length:* 78.4 cm
Length of cross: 8.7 cm *Length of grip:* 9.9 cm
Balance point: 16.5 cm
Condition: blade in excavated condition with a hole close to the hilt; hilt is good

The museum entry for this sword states that it came to the museum on October 1st, 1942 and was found in a small river in the old ford between Heining and Naesby: 'Found when a digging machine unearthed them'.[1] It was recorded to have been found with an antler cheek-piece and this may well be an unrelated find.

This is yet again an excellent example of a single-edged weapon and comparable to the condition and quality of C24550, also from Copenhagen and shown on pp. 50–51. The long blade, which has lost an estimated 3 cm of its tip, shows no evidence of pattern-welding or inscription. It has a straight sort of grain, parallel to the length of the blade and bears some focal delaminated areas, suggestive of slag inclusions.

Again, this is a prestige weapon, the appearance of the hilt elements being strikingly similar to C24550, in terms of both the nature of the applied decoration and the degree of wear.[2] The lateral faces of the crossguard are decorated with inlaid brass, in parallel strips in line with the length of the blade. The upper and lower faces of the classically boat-shaped crossguard still retain a thinly applied plate of brass, the lower face being almost intact.[3] Both the upper guard and the pommel have decoration similar to that seen on the cross, with an estimated 60 to 70% of the decoration intact on one side and almost all in place on the other. The lower face of the upper guard is sheathed in an almost complete applied plate of brass, pierced by the two rivets which hold the upper guard and pommel together. Upon its completion, sometime in the late ninth century, this sword and its partner C24550 must have been viewed with reverential wonder with their burnished blades and golden coloured hilts.

In contrast, the single-edged examples excavated at the Island-Bridge and Kilmainham sites in Dublin have undecorated and much more angular hilts, as can be seen in Plunket's nineteenth century watercolour.[4]

[1] This entry seems to imply that other artifacts were also unearthed.
[2] Compared with sword C24550 the decoration on the hilt is not so intact but still retains some 80% of the original coverage.
[3] These plates may well have been of gold; certainly their colour bore no relationship to the other applied decoration on the hilt.
[4] See NM6245A:1 from Helsinki on pp. 60–62 for further details on this type.

← Copenhagen C24554 full length view. Photograph courtesy of and copyright National Museum of Denmark, negative III 359.

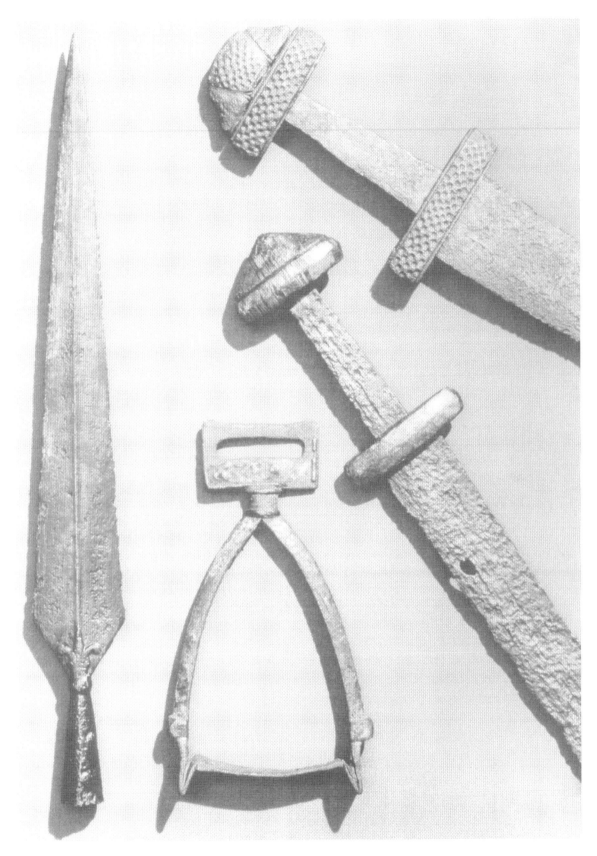

↑ Assemblage of Viking Age artifacts. Copenhagen C24554 is the lower sword. The upper sword is of Petersen's type E. The other artifacts were *not* found with C24554. Photograph courtesy of and copyright National Museum of Denmark.

Date: ninth century
Find-place: Sørup, Måløv, Smørum, København, Denmark
Overall length: 90.0 cm *Blade length:* 74.3 cm
Length of cross: 8.3 cm *Length of grip:* 9.2 cm
Balance point: 16.5 cm
Condition: the hilt is in a fine state of preservation, retaining all applied decoration; the blade is in a reasonably good excavated condition; the durability of the applied decorative elements is remarkable

The museum entry is for 1942 when 'in June of that year a site was inspected' and objects collected. The finder was a labourer called Caspelsen. The sword was found lying horizontally in a peat bog with two bundles of arrow heads either side [I think we may read this as two bundles of arrows].

This is a good example of a single-edged weapon, the blade surviving in a fairly reasonable excavated condition. A small portion of the point is missing, perhaps some 3 cm, which would have brought the original blade length up to some 77 cm. There are no visual traces of pattern-welding or inlays of any kind, a feature not unexpected with single-edged sword blades in the Viking Age. Such single-edged sword blades are usually regarded as being the work of a local smith, rather than being imported from a specialized workshop. Such blades tend to be thicker and thus heavier, explaining the rather forward balance point observed in this example.

The hilt of this weapon is not unlike the remains of a beautifully decorated sword, recovered from a bulldozer site at Island-Bridge but originating from the Viking John's Lane-Fishamble Street site in Dublin.[1] The guards and pommel of the Copenhagen sword are covered with latten or brass applied as fine strips or wires parallel to the length of the blade, each strip being some 0.05 cm wide. There is no doubt that the original intention was decoration as an unbroken film of latten over all elements of the hilt and, although some is missing, the effect is even now highly impressive. A flat plate of latten also covers both the upper and lower faces of the crossguard and indeed the face of the upper guard adjacent to the grip. A portion of lined pattern with exposure of the underlying ferrous metal is noticeable over the high points of both of the guards and the pommel and would appear to be the result of abrasive wear in antiquity, as opposed to corrosion.

It is worth repeating what Petersen stated regarding type H: 'This type holds an exceptional position due to the broad time period it extends across.' It is, he further states, the most numerous of all the sword types from the Viking Age.[2]

[1] See in particular *From Viking to Crusader: The Scandinavians and Europe 800 to 1200* (22nd Council of Europe Exhibition) (Copenhagen, 1992), cat. no. 387, p. 329. See also the weapon illustrated in the article written by George Coffey and E.C.R. Armstrong, 'Scandinavian Objects Found at Island-Bridge and Kilmainham', *Proceedings of the Royal Irish Academy* vol. XXVIII, sect. C (1910), pp. 107–122.
[2] See Jan Petersen, *De Norske Vikingesverd* (Oslo, 1919), pp. 89–101 and NM 6245A:1 on pp. 60–62 which includes a long discussion on type H.

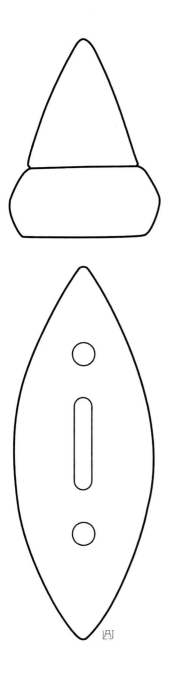

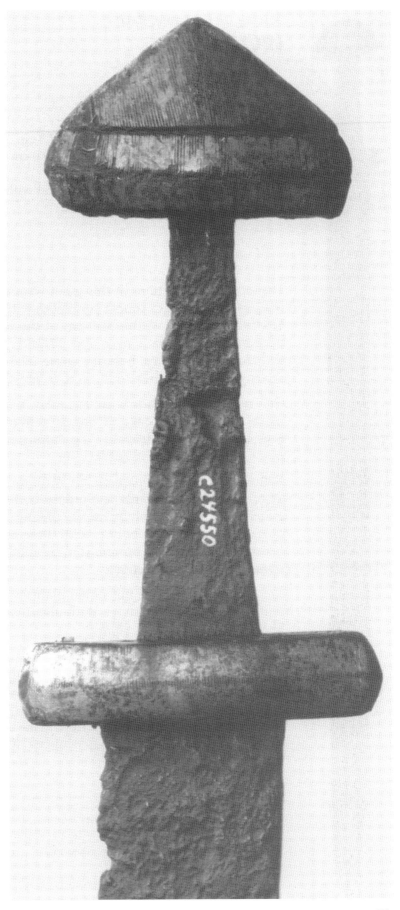

↑ Diagram of a type H pommel and upper guard from fig. 79 of Petersen showing a pommel and upper guard viewed from the end and the profile of the upper guard from below with positions for insertion of the tang and the rivets which secure the pommel to the upper guard.

← Copenhagen C24550 full length view. Photograph courtesy of and copyright by the National Museum of Denmark, negative III 339.

→ Copenhagen C24550 detail of hilt. Photograph courtesy of and copyright by the National Museum of Denmark, negative I 2202.

Date: late ninth century
Overall length: 94.8 cm *Blade length:* 78.3 cm
Length of cross: 7.7 cm *Length of grip:* 10.0 cm
Balance point: 18.7 cm
Condition: hilt excellent, blade very good with some areas in pristine condition

The slender proportions of this great weapon from the late ninth century are alluring, with its cutting edges almost parallel to within a few centimetres of the rounded point.[1] The fullers run to within 13.0 cm of the business-end and there is a quite unusual thickening of the blade over that distance. The blade has been broken and nicely re-welded (in antiquity, I think) some 27.5 cm from the cross. This weld has been accomplished with great skill, so as to prevent breaking the imposing line of the blade.

On one side of the blade is an iron inlay in the form of a giant snake running down the fuller for some 29.0 cm and hugely reminiscent of a broken bladed sword I closely inspected in 1994 in Helsinki.[2] The cutting edges are massively wide and thick and bear much evidence of use in battle.

Both the cross and the pommel are in an excellent state of preservation, boasting almost all of their original surface and indeed both are unusually slim in character. There is no evidence of silver, latten or bronze plating upon either the cross or pommel, unlike so many of the surviving swords with these hilt types.[3] There is however a small piece of decoration, a thin but pronounced, beaded iron wire separating both elements of the pommel and most effectively.

The more I contemplate this rather plain sword, with its long grip and massive tang, the more I become aware that it is undoubtedly one of the finest to have endured the rigours of time.[4]

[1] This adjective alone came to mind when handling this very special sword in July 1995.
[2] Jorma Leppäaho, *Späteisenzeitliche Waffen aus Finnland: Schwertinschriften und Waffenverzierungen des 9.–12. Jahrhunderts* (Helsinki, 1964), p. 68 and pl. 32.
[3] See, in particular, the swords described in the Copenhagen collection (pp. 48–51 herein).
[4] Of all the hundreds of Viking Age weapons I have had the honour to handle, this weapon must come within the top ten.

→ Hilt of JPO 2249 showing guards with a bevelled face having a central ridge; generally an early feature in a type H hilt. The lack of applied surface decoration and the beaded band separating pommel and upper guard are unusual but not unique. Photograph courtesy of and copyright Musée de l'Armée, Paris, negative K23715.

← Full length view of JPO 2249 showing the well-defined fuller. Photograph courtesy of and copyright Musée de l'Armée, Paris, negative K23714.

53

NM 18402:1

Date: ninth century
Find-place: Peltorinne, Hämeenlinna (Tavastehus), Häme, Finland
Overall length: 91.6 cm *Blade length:* 76.2 cm
Length of cross: 10.5 cm *Length of grip:* 8.9 cm
Balance point: 11.2 cm
Condition: good with some light pitting, hilt and blade covered in a patchy black patina

This is truly one of the greatest swords to have come down to us. It is clear that the swordsmith, a gifted craftsman in his own right, had recognized how wieldability could be greatly enhanced by a blade design with a centre of gravity close to the hilt. The acute tapering of the blade towards the point, the wide fullers and the bulky pommel all fit an equation most beneficial to the user. Both fullers run to within 4.5 cm of the spatulate shaped point and each cutting edge remains well defined. It may well be that this blade was broken or required reinforcement and was welded in antiquity. It is also slightly bent out of true at a point some 18 cm from the crossguard. The reputation of this prestige weapon is further enhanced by the presence of a fine Ulfberht inscription on one side of the blade. The sprawling irregular, but exciting, letters are inlaid in pattern-welded iron and must have added much to the startling appearance of this weapon during its period of active use. The inscription reads **+VLFBERHT+**. On the reverse side of the blade is a typical example of Ulfberht's decoration, but it appears to be incomplete when compared with other examples.[1] The tang is sturdy and robust as one would expect with such a noble and well-balanced weapon. The black patina points most strongly to this weapon being a river-find. Indeed, the blade and hilt appear to have not been subjected to any form of cleaning.

The crossguard is decorated on the lateral faces with fine strands of copper and silver wire hammered into cuts on the surface of the parent metal and although mostly covered by the black patina it is still possible to define the pattern of decoration as chequerboard. The upper and lower faces of the crossguard still retain substantial fragments of an applied plate of latten. The upper guard bears minute traces of silver wire and appears to be separated from the pommel by a thin metal plate. The pommel also retains isolated traces of latten or bronze wire. All wire decoration runs in line with the blade.[2]

In every respect this is an outstanding sword, and one may reasonably assume that it was made for, or at least used by, a very notable warrior. The shape and proportions of the massive hilt are closely akin to a similar sword, from a male grave found at Zaozere (mound 6), SE Ladoga region, Russia and bearing the iron-inlaid inscription **CEROLT**.[3]

[1] For numerous Ulfberht inscriptions, see especially Jorma Leppäaho, *Späteisenzeitliche Waffen aus Finnland: Schwertinschriften und Waffenverzierungen des 9.–12. Jahrhunderts* (Helsinki, 1964), pp. 34–47. Some thirty to forty examples with the name Ulfberht are known in Finland.
[2] For a similar type of weapon, see the splendid example from the Kilmainham Island-Bridge site, Dublin, now in the National Museum of Ireland, registration no. 1933:7-15. See also Johs. Bøe, 'Norse Antiquities in Ireland', *Viking Antiquities in Great Britain and Ireland, Part III*, ed. Haakon Shetelig (Oslo, 1940), pp. 62–65.
[3] *From Viking to Crusader: The Scandinavians and Europe 800 to 1200* (22nd Council of Europe Exhibition) (Copenhagen, 1992), cat. no. 294, pp. 304–305.

← Helsinki 18402:1 full length view. Photograph by H. Malmgreer (1972) courtesy of and copyright National Museum of Finland, negative 38117.

→ Helsinki 18402:1 detail of hilt. Photograph by Ritva Bäckman (1996) courtesy of and copyright National Museum of Finland.

↓ Schematic of inlays of copper (darker) and silver (lighter) on the guards of Helsinki 18402:1.

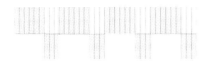

↓ Detail of Ulfberht inscription on 18402:1. Photograph by Ritva Bäckman (1996) courtesy of and copyright National Museum of Finland.

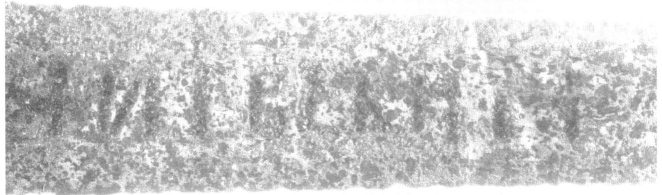

Date: ninth century
Find-place: Dungolman River, Parish of Rathconrath, County West Meath, Ireland
Overall length: 92.0 cm *Blade length:* 77.3 cm
Length of cross: 9.2 cm *Length of grip:* 8.6 cm
Balance point: 14.5 cm
Condition: both hilt and blade in a fine state of preservation

Wakeman stated that 'This is the best-preserved sword of its class in the collection and is strong and sharp enough to be used in the present day. Found in a depression in the bed of the Dungolman River, in the townland of Dungolman, parish of Rathconrath, County West Meath. Presented by the Board of Works.'

This fine weapon is, indeed, in a sound state of preservation. The long, finely tapered blade carries well-defined fullers, which run to within 10.0 cm of the point. The broad cutting edges are still well defined and Bøe is correct in stating that the blade had been reground in modern times, perhaps at the hand of the finder.[1] There is a slight curve (1.0 cm out of true) to the blade, but this is hardly perceptible.[2]

A close visual examination of this blade did not reveal any positive evidence of inlay or decoration of any kind, although it is a worthy candidate for x-ray examination in the future. On one side of the blade, along some 6 inches of the fuller and close to the hilt, is a corroded zone which makes it possible to conclude that the blade is pattern-welded. The fullers continue for about 2.0 cm along the broad, hefty tang.

The boat-shaped cross still retains considerable qualities of decoration on one lateral face in the form of alternating strips of silver and bronze wire hammered onto the parent metal.[3] There are also a few square centimetres of thin silver plate attached to the grip side of the cross.

The lower part of the pommel mirrors the shape of the cross. Many areas of the pommel still retain vertical strips of silver wire hammered onto the surface and, like the cross, the flat underside adjacent to the grip still boasts considerable remains of a plate of sheet silver.

The shallow groove separating the upper and lower portions of the pommel is empty, but at one time, almost certainly contained a silver wire.

Sufficient decoration remains for us to close our eyes and attempt to visualize the wondrous appearance of this silver and bronze bedecked weapon, as it appeared to its owner sometime in the ninth century.

[1] Johs. Bøe, 'Norse Antiquities in Ireland', *Viking Antiquities in Great Britain and Ireland, Part III*, ed. Haakon Shetelig (Oslo, 1940), p. 83 and fig. 53a. The width of the blade at the cross is 5.3 cm.
[2] Due almost certainly to uneven amounts of corrosion on each side of the blade, as a result of immersion in the river bed
[3] Museum records reveal that one person who examined this sword thought that he detected traces of gilding on the cross and pommel. When I examined this weapon in 1994, I saw no such traces.

← Full length view of WK-24. Photograph courtesy of and copyright National Museum of Ireland.

→ Hilt of WK-24, showing the remaining traces of silver and copper wire upon the crossguard and some residual applied silver wire on the upper guard and pommel. Photograph courtesy of and copyright National Museum of Ireland.

Date: ninth century
Find-place: cemetery at Island-Bridge and Kilmainham, Ireland, on January 19, 1866
Overall length: 96.8 cm   *Blade length:* 79.3 cm
Length of cross: 11.5 cm   *Length of grip:* 9.1 cm
Condition: blade in a poor excavated condition; hilt and decoration remarkably well preserved

The main part of the cemetery at Island-Bridge and Kilmainham was destroyed about the middle of the nineteenth century when digging began on the foundations for the Kilmainham Hospital and for the railway line at Island-Bridge. This beautifully decorated sword came from that cemetery, where a great part of the grave goods passed unnoticed by the workers and were consequently lost.[1]

It also is certain that not all of the objects which were actually found by the workers came into the possession of the Royal Irish Academy, whose collection is now housed in the National Museum.

According to Bøe, this wonderful ninth century weapon appeared to have been treated with strong caustic and has consequently suffered, as a result.[2]

The boat-shaped cross is decorated with 1.0 mm wide vertical strips of silver wire alternating with the iron of the parent metal. The effect is dazzling.[3] There are bronze plates applied to both the flat surfaces of the cross. They are both intact and firmly in place.

Both the upper and lower elements of the pommel are decorated in a similar manner to the cross, and it is here that we can see the devastating, damaging effects of the application of a caustic solution. The decoration is strikingly similar to the sword recovered from a bulldozer dump at Island-Bridge but originating from the John's Lane–Fishamble Street Site.[4]

To add to the decorative appearance of the hilt, a twisted silver wire has been forced into the groove between the upper and lower elements of the pommel. The under flat surface of the pommel also bears a plate of bronze, still firmly attached, which is pierced by two rivets, holding the upper and lower parts of the pommel together.

The blade is in a very poor state and broken in two places. According to Bøe, in Wakeman's time there was apparently only one break.

[1] See Johs. Bøe, 'Norse Antiquities in Ireland', *Viking Antiquities in Great Britain and Ireland, Part III*, ed. Haakon Shetelig (Oslo, 1940), p. 11.
[2] Ibid., p. 16 and fig. 2, p. 15.
[3] See illustration of whole sword taken after the silver had been cleaned. See also George Coffey and E.C.R. Armstrong, 'Scandinavian Objects Found at Island-Bridge and Kilmainham', *Proceedings of the Royal Irish Academy* vol. XXVIII, sect. C (1910), pp. 107–122, and pl. IV. fig. 1.
[4] *From Viking to Crusader: The Scandinavians and Europe 800 to 1200* (22nd Council of Europe Exhibition) (Copenhagen, 1992), p. 329, cat. no. 387.

← Full length view of WK-21. Photograph courtesy of and copyright National Museum of Ireland.

→ Hilt of WK-21, showing the remaining applied silver decoration including a twisted silver wire between the upper guard and pommel. Photograph courtesy of and copyright National Museum of Ireland.

Date: late ninth to early tenth century
Find-place: Kangasala, Tiihala, Jussila, Finland
Overall length: 84.7 cm *Blade length:* 72.2 cm (incomplete)
Length of cross: 10.0 cm *Length of grip:* 8.2 cm
Balance point: 17.5 cm
Condition: good, some heavy pitting on the blade, yet with some portions in almost pristine condition; much of the decoration remains on the hilt.

Close consideration of the proportions of this superb specimen which dates from circa 900 reveals that it has probably lost some 5 cm (two inches) of its tip, and yet, apart from some deep pitting, it remains in an excellent excavated state of preservation. In character, it is similar to the sword in the National Museum of Ireland, Dublin, recovered from a bulldozer dump at Island-Bridge and originating from the John's Lane–Fishamble Street site[1] and to another from the same collection, emanating from one of the few excavated graves from the Kilmainham Island-Bridge cemetery.[2] Both date from the 9th century.

The well defined fullers taper from 2.9 cm wide at the cross to some 1.8 cm approaching the distal end. The cutting edges are, again, in an excellent state of preservation and indeed, almost pristine in some areas. The blade is bent, whether by accident or intention, at a point approximately 30 cm from the cross and to a degree of some 5.3 cm out of true. On one side the fuller contains a clear **INGELRII** inscription and almost all of the inlay is intact.[3] Leppäaho informs us that the inscription 'in threefold damascene steps, appeared by grinding, polishing and oxidizing with water'.[4] The reverse side of the blade bears ornamentation in the form of an 'x'-like device between two groups of parallel bars as illustrated on the opposite page. The tang is massively robust, running from 2.6 to 2.3 cm in width and is a clear indication that the warrior and or bladesmith, whether independently or in collusion, had realized that tremendous stresses were exerted upon the junction of the blade and tang when in use, and had modified the tang size to combat these stresses.

The simple elliptical cross is handsomely decorated by bands of copper sandwiched between two shorter bands of silver and much of this extremely effective decoration remains. The upper guard is decorated in a similar fashion, but retains more silver and copper inlay than the cross. It is pierced by two holes which would have taken the rivets holding the pommel firmly in place. There is no certain way of discerning the pommel type, but there are strong hints that we have the remains of a Petersen type H.

Petersen insists that this type holds an important position, due to the broad time period across which it extends. It is also the most numerous of all the sword types from the Viking Age and up until the publication of his book, he was aware that 213 specimens had been found in Norway, 142 with double-edged blades, 52 with single-edged blades and 19 which were undetermined. South and North Trondhjem and Stavanger produced the most finds with 25, 20 and 24 respectively.[5] Petersen further lists other characteristics of the type, namely that the cross and upper guard are especially wide, so that even when the pommel has fallen off and is missing in a find, type identification can be made by the massive width of the upper guard and by the striped ornamentation present.[6] This ornamentation takes the form of thin silver, bronze, copper or occasionally brass plates. Quite commonly there are different decorative metals on the same sword, with for example, silver and copper interwoven into simple geometric figures. Most commonly, the coating was built up using bronze or copper wires, but as we have seen, silver was also often used.

Many type H swords have 'damascened' blades, several of which have inscriptions, and Lorange illustrates two examples of this type with Ulfberht inscriptions.[7]

[1] *From Viking to Crusader: The Scandinavians and Europe 800 to 1200* (22nd Council of Europe Exhibition) (Copenhagen, 1992), cat. no. 389 and registration number 1979:68 in the National Museum of Ireland. Apparently, this is an early type not found elsewhere on excavated urban sites in Ireland.

[2] *From Viking to Crusader*, cat. no. 354 and registration number 1933:7-15 in the National Museum of Ireland. As already mentioned, this sword is one of a group of objects found in one of the few excavated graves from the Kilmainham Island-Bridge cemetery. The sword, together with the axe and spearhead are all of Scandinavian origin and typical of those found in Viking graves in Western Europe. See also Johs. Bøe, 'Norse Antiquities in Ireland', *Viking Antiquities in Great Britain and Ireland, Part III*, ed. Haakon Shetelig (Oslo, 1940), pp. 62–65.

[3] The inscription appears to have been enhanced by outlining the letters in orange marker for exhibition purposes, but is most likely the result of the application of etching fluids.

[4] Jorma Leppäaho, *Späteisenzeitliche Waffen aus Finnland: Schwertinschriften und Waffenverzierungen des 9.–12. Jahrhunderts* (Helsinki, 1964), p. 34.

[5] Petersen accumulated much information on his type H. See especially Jan Petersen, *De Norske Vikingesverd* (Oslo, 1919), pp. 91–101.

[6] According to Jan Petersen the precious metal or metals was hammered onto the parent metal, the surface of which had been previously prepared with a grid of fine scratches.

[7] A. L. Lorange, *Den Yngre Jernalders Sværd* (Bergen, 1889), see Sword B2944 from Sundalen, Dale, S. Holmedal, tab. I, fig. 2a and sword B1483 from Visnæs, Stryn, Nordfjord, tab. I, fig. 4 (found in 1861), reproduced herein as plate III.

↑ Helsinki 6245A:1 photograph of blade inscription. Photograph by E. Laakso (1958) courtesy of and copyright by the National Museum of Finland, negative 21265, previously published in Leppäaho, p. 35, pl. 15, 1c.

↓ Helsinki 6245A:1 schematic of iron-inlaid inscription on the opposite face of the blade.

← Helsinki 6245A:1 full length view. Photograph courtesy of and copyright National Museum of Finland, negative 28156.

illustrations continue overleaf →

↑ Helsinki 6245A:1 detail of hilt. Photograph by E. Laakso (1955) courtesy of and copyright National Museum of Finland, negative 18681, previously published in Leppäaho, p. 35, pl. 15, 1a.

Date: ninth century
Find-place: Ballinderry bog drainage ditch, Ireland
Overall length: 92.8 cm *Blade length:* 79 cm
Length of cross: 11.0 cm *Length of grip:* 8.5 cm
Balance point: 18.5 cm
Condition: excellent

This prestigious weapon is the finest and indeed the most important to be found in Ireland. It is one of a family of five surviving swords with similarly inscribed hilts.

Details of its find-place are therefore equally important. It was found in 1928 'in the drainage ditch that drains Ballinderry Bog' while it was being cleaned by the Board of Works.

The Museum record states that 'the crannog was discovered in May 1928 when the "river" or large drainage ditch that drains Ballinderry Bog and divides the townlands of Kilnahinch and Ballinderry was cleaned by the Board of Works. At that time a man in their employ, Richard Greene, found a sword in the bed of the stream… Dr. Marh… visited the scene… and also found animal bones, part of a bone comb and timbers in the sides of the drain and at once recognized that the site was a hitherto unknown crannog.'[1]

Further records state 'objects found on the floor of House 1… Iron, Viking Sword. This remarkable weapon, the finest of its kind found thus far in Ireland, was discovered… in all probability upon the floor of house 1. According to Greene, he found the point of the sword sticking up in the bottom of the drain with its hilt embedded in marl.'

The blade of this ninth or tenth century weapon is most beautifully shaped with the cutting edges perfectly preserved in places, as indeed are the fullers. Large areas of the blade are in almost pristine condition, boasting their original surface. It bears an **+ULFBERHT+** inscription with the iron inlay of a pattern-welded form, identical to those illustrated by Lorange.[2] The reverse side has a typical design long associated with Ulfberht, three 'X' characters between single parallel bars (**IXXXI**).[3] The blade does not otherwise appear to be pattern-welded.

In contrast to the Wallace sword, one of a family of five,[4] all elements of the hilt of the Ballinderry weapon are encased in silver. The precious metal has been applied by covering the surface of the iron with tiny parallel incisions, onto which the silver sheets were placed and hammered. The decoration was then completed by cutting through the silver to reveal the iron below. Both sides of the cross are ornamented with a stylized vine scroll reminiscent of that on the Wallace sword and indeed a sword from Malhus, Norway, whose blade also carries an Ulfberht inscription.

The upper side of the cross bears the **HILTIPREHT** inscription, which has been most exquisitely executed and remains almost as clear as the day it was formed. It is identical, apart from the size of lettering, to that on the cross of the sword from Malhus, with many hints of it being the work of the same craftsman.[5]

→ Full length view of 1928:382. Photograph courtesy of and copyright National Museum of Ireland.

Each end of the lower side of the cross is decorated with a device, similar to the erect ears of a rabbit and a single similar device may be seen on one end of the Wallace cross. The five-lobed pommel retains much of its silver plating and the lower element has a similar vine scroll decoration without the grapes.

A portion of the cutting edge, some 17.0 cm from the cross, shows that the blade was originally extremely wide for a considerable part of its length. The tang is sturdy and robust, and sufficiently so to support such a massively wide blade.

Other finds from the crannog were two fine spearheads (one illustrated), a well-preserved and complete axehead and a gaming board of yew wood.[6]

[1] This weapon is described and illustrated in Adolf Mahr, 'Ein Wikinger Schwert Mit Deutschem Namen Aus Irland', *Mannus* VI. Ergänzungsband, p. 240. See in particular Ewart Oakeshott and Ian Peirce, 'Hiltipreht! Name Or Invocation', *Park Lane Arms Fair Catalogue* 12 (1995), pp. 6–11.
[2] For other examples of this type of inlay, see Jorma Leppäaho, *Späteisenzeitliche Waffen aus Finnland: Schwertinschriften und Waffenverzierungen des 9.–12. Jahrhunderts* (Helsinki, 1964), pp. 7, 9, 37, 43 and 47 and A.L. Lorange, *Den Yngre Jernalders Svaerd* (Bergen, 1889), pl. 1, 2, 3, 4 and 5.
[3] There are variations in the design on the reverse side of Ulfberht blades. On occasion the three 'X's may be flanked by groups of one, two or three upright bars. Yet again, the three 'X's may be replaced by a lattice work pattern again flanked by either one, two or three upright bars.
[4] See also the grid comparing the five swords bearing cross inscriptions, from the Wallace Collection, Ballinderry, Berlin, Malhus, and Kilmainham in Ewart Oakeshott and Ian Peirce, 'Hiltipreht! Name Or Invocation', *Park Lane Arms Fair Catalogue* 12 (1995), p. 6.
[5] Sir James Mann, *Wallace Collection Catalogs: European Arms & Armour, Vol. II* (London, 1962), pp. 240–241 states that the inscription on the Malhus sword is **HLITER**. From my recent investigations, this is clearly wrong.
[6] See Johs. Bøe, 'Norse Antiquities in Ireland', *Viking Antiquities in Great Britain and Ireland, Part III*, ed. Haakon Shetelig (Oslo, 1940), pp. 77–79 for more detail. See also Mann, vol. II, pp. 240–241 and H. R. Ellis Davidson, *The Sword in Anglo-Saxon England* (Oxford, 1962), plate IIb, IIc and plate IVa.

↑ Detail of the **+VLFBERHT+** inscription. Photograph courtesy of and copyright National Museum of Ireland.

→ Details of the silver hilt decoration. Photograph courtesy of and copyright National Museum of Ireland.

↓ One of 2 spears found in the Ballinderry Crannog. Photograph courtesy of and copyright National Museum of Ireland.

← Full length view of J1 showing the gently tapering and spatulate tipped blade with its wide fuller. Photograph courtesy of and copyright Musée de l'Armée, Paris, negative K23716.

→ Hilt of J1 showing plain guards and a pommel with seven lobes, each once separated from another by twisted silver wire. Photograph courtesy of and copyright Musée de l'Armée, Paris, negative K23717.

Universitetets Oldsaksamling, Oslo
C11014

Date: late ninth century
Find-place: Kilde farm, Åmot, Hedemark, Norway
Overall length: 94.5 cm *Blade length:* 79.8 cm
Length of cross: 11.7 cm *Length of grip:* 9.2 cm
Balance point: 17.5 cm
Condition: excellent

This sword was found in a field of Kilde farm, Åmot, Hedemark, near to some grave mounds with a spear, a double-bladed arrow, a knife, a sax (26.3 cm long),[1] a sickle and belt fitments in iron; all surrounded by black earth where traces of bones were in evidence. Some areas of the blade and hilt are covered in a quite unusual surface bubbling. It is very similar to the appearance of many river finds prior to conservation and may well be due to the chemical nature of the earth in which the grave was dug.[2]

The blade on this ninth century weapon is in excellent condition with large areas in almost pristine condition, though it is slightly bent out of line in two places, one some 17 cm from the cross and again at a point 30 cm from the tip. The cutting edges are almost as sound as the day they were formed and each occupies almost one third of the width of the stout, finely proportioned blade.[3] The fullers also have excellent definition and run to within some 5 cm of the tip. Quite unusually, the tip is perfectly preserved.

The well preserved, stub-ended boat-shaped cross has no apparent form of decoration except for a single thin groove cut along each edge of the lateral faces, thus making a very simple but effective form of decoration. The massive pommel, although quite in keeping with all other elements of this weapon, has 5 lobes, the central one being the largest, and is securely fastened to the stout tang.[4] The pommel has been forged in one piece and is divided around its girth by two parallel grooves with yet another pair of grooves at the lower edge. The cross-section of the pommel is slightly more boat-shaped than the cross.

Without a doubt this is one of the finest surviving weapons of this age.[5]

---

[1] *Sax* can also mean scissors according to my translator.
[2] There is no evidence that this weapon has ever been cleaned.
[3] Lee Jones and I both handled this fine weapon in 1993.
[4] It is indeed massive; compare with the pommels in fig. 89 and fig. 90 in Jan Petersen, *De Norske Vikingesverd* (Oslo, 1919).
[5] For several other swords of this type, see Ewart Oakeshott and Ian Peirce, 'Hiltipreht! Name or Invocation', *Park Lane Arms Fair Catalogue* 12 (1995), pp. 6–11.

← Full length view of C11014 showing the especially well defined fuller. Photograph by Ove Holst courtesy of and copyright Universitetets Oldsaksamling, negative 22343a.

↗ The outlines of the pommel from the side and below are adapted from fig. 91 of Jan Petersen, *De Norske Vikingesverd* (Oslo, 1919), p. 107, which is an illustration of this hilt.

→ Hilt of C11014 showing the simple scribed decoration. Photograph by Eirik Irgens Johnsen courtesy of and copyright Universitetets Oldsaksamling, negative 23352/13.

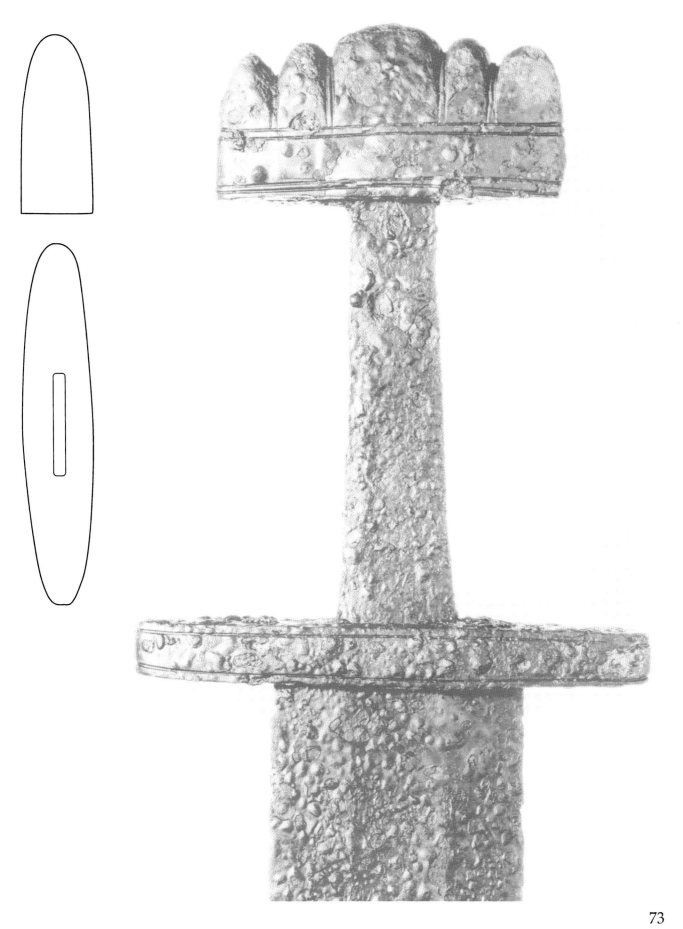

73

Date: mid ninth to mid tenth century
Overall length: 88.3 cm *Blade length:* 76.4 cm
Length of cross: 9.0 cm *Length of grip:* 7.9 cm
Balance point: 22.6 cm
Condition: some heavy pitting but good in places

The sword under examination is a Petersen type L and it has been stated so much in the past that this is an English hilt type. It is true that a few examples have been found in the British Isles and England, in particular, but not as many as in Norway.[1] Jan Petersen lists fourteen in his Sword Register and they are spread over a wide area of find places.[2] It is of mid ninth to mid tenth century.

Occasionally, perhaps even more frequently, and especially in the light of new data, we should be open to adjusting our thoughts and opinions on certain topics. I, therefore, believe that we must now consider Petersen type L as a Viking (Scandinavian) type hilt frequently found (and therefore likely popular) in England.

This good example from Paris is most definitely a river find, such identification being possible due to the jet-black nature of its surface, both on the blade and the hilt.[3]

The blade is broad (6.0 cm at the hilt) and, most unusually, carries wide deep fullers all the way through to the point which shows slight damage.

The cross curves gracefully towards the blade and still has small pieces of silver adhering to its edges. There is still a portion of the wooden grip attached to the cross and tang (see close-up of hilt). A simple plain iron ferrule or collar remains freely attached to the sturdy tang. This would have originally overlaid the pommel end of the grip.

There are also traces of silver on both the upper and lower elements of the trilobated pommel. A beaded strip or solid wire of either silver or iron would have originally separated these, but this has been lost. Some decoration has survived on either side of the remaining channel that would have carried the iron or silver wire, in the form of a serrated pattern, running around the periphery of the pommel.

This must have been a strikingly beautiful weapon in its youth, especially as it appears as though all parts of the hilt were silver plated.

One similar sword from Lempälä, Finland, illustrated by Jorma Leppäaho, has some iron inlay on the blade: on one side a cross flanked by two omegas and upon the other side a cross potent followed by a swirl of inlay, much like a whirlpool.[4] It may well be that this Paris blade also has some iron inlay.

---

[1] See H.R. Ellis Davidson, *The Sword in Anglo-Saxon England* (Oxford, 1962), pl. X. It is strikingly similar to no. 66, the sword found in the River Witham and now in the Sheffield Museum. The blade of this example is pattern-welded.
[2] See especially Jan Petersen, *De Norske Vikingesverd* (Oslo, 1919), figs. 94, 95, 96 and 97.
[3] There is also another type L in Paris in the Musée National du Moyen Âge - Thermes et Hôtel de Cluny, museum no. CL 11060.
[4] Jorma Leppäaho, *Späteisenzeitliche Waffen aus Finnland: Schwertinschriften und Waffenverzierungen des 9.–12. Jahrhunderts* (Helsinki, 1964), p. 24, sword no. NM 1996:73.

→ Hilt of JPO 2262 showing guards strongly curving away from the grip, characteristic of Petersen's type L. Photograph courtesy of and copyright Musée de l'Armée, Paris, negative K23709.

← Full length view of JPO 2262 showing a gently tapering blade with the fuller extending almost to the tip, suggesting the possibility that this sword was once shortened. Photograph courtesy of and copyright Musée de l'Armée, Paris, negative K23708.

Date: mid ninth to mid tenth century
Find-place: stream bank near Hurbuck, Durham, England
Overall length: 88 cm *Blade length:* 74.4 cm
Length of cross: 8.3 cm *Length of grip:* 8.0 cm
Balance point: 22.1 cm
Condition: both blade and hilt are heavily corroded

According to the museum register, this sword was found at Hurbuck, Durham in a stream bank and was part of a hoard purchased from the Rev. William Greenwell.

The tapered blade of this late ninth century Anglo-Saxon sword is badly corroded upon both sides and for most of its length, but this does allow us, with great clarity, to view the structure. The blade is one of the thickest I have ever handled and there is faint evidence of a wide fuller which is 3 cm wide at the crossguard end. The blade is much better preserved from the midpoint to the hilt and the cutting edges are prominent over this portion, as well. At a point some 20 cm from the cross, the blade is bent approximately 2.5 cm out of true and again at a distance of some 45 cm from the crossguard, but in the opposite direction. I do not think this sword had been ritually killed. The huge tang is tapered in both width and thickness towards the pommel. The radiographic tests carried out on the blade revealed two layers consisting of three continuously twisting bands, not completely superimposed. The bands have a longer twist at intervals, and have been arranged to coincide across the width.[1]

The boat-shaped crossguard is about 0.6 cm thick, curves gently towards the blade and has small traces of silver clinging to it. The upper guard is a smaller copy of the crossguard and is surmounted by a delightful little three lobed pommel which is badly corroded and which consequently bears no trace of surviving applied precious metal.

A sword with a similar hilt was found in the River Witham at Fiskerton and is now in the Sheffield Museum. Yet another good example is that from the Thames.[2] Leslie Webster of the British Museum has described the Fiskerton sword as follows:

> Two edged iron sword with silver mounted hilt. The blade is pattern-welded; the hilt consists of a grip (originally with an organic covering) with three decorated bands, curved guards and a silver-mounted pommel with central lobed element flanked by twin stylised animal-head shoulders. The rather crudely-decorated Trewhiddle-style silver mounts on grip and pommel are inlaid with niello, the former entirely with geometric and plant ornament, the latter with geometric and animal ornament.[3]

Wheeler suggested that this style of hilt originated in England as the splendid Abingdon hilt appeared from the decoration to be Anglo-Saxon work.[4]

[1] See Janet Lang and Barry Ager, 'Swords of the Anglo-Saxon and Viking Periods in the British Museum: a Radiographic Study', *Weapons and Warfare in Anglo-Saxon England*, ed. Sonia Chadwick Hawkes (Oxford, 1989), p. 99. See also fig. 7, 3c on p. 90.
[2] See H.R. Ellis Davidson, *The Sword in Anglo-Saxon England* (Oxford, 1962), pl. X and figs. 66 and 68, respectively.
[3] See also Leslie Webster and Janet Backhouse, *The Making of England: Anglo-Saxon Art and Culture AD 600–900* (London, 1991), p. 276.
[4] See Davidson, pp. 55–56.

← Full length view of 1912, 7-23 1. Photograph courtesy of and copyright British Museum.

Date: tenth century
Find-place: River Witham opposite Monks Abbey, Lincoln, England
Overall length: 91.5 cm *Blade length:* 77.8 cm
Length of cross: 11.8 cm *Length of grip:* 8.8 cm
Balance point: 17.4 cm
Condition: all elements of this superb specimen are in an excellent state of preservation

This weapon would 'upstage' virtually all of the swords in the best public and private collections of the world. It was found in October 1848 and presented to the British Museum by J. Hayward, Esquire of Beaumont Manor, Lincoln. 'The sword was stated to have been found during widening of the river Witham opposite Monks Abbey, Lincoln.'[1]

The beautifully tapered blade has received virtually no corrosion, being protected by the buildup of a black scale which contains principally goethite ($FeO(OH)$). The blade is a little more than 6 cm wide where it meets the crossguard. The bold, well-defined fullers are 2.9 cm wide at their origin and 1.4 cm wide at the extreme end where they run to within 8 cm of the point. Over the last 12 cm the blade curves delicately into the decorated cross. The blade of this sword is completely straight and carries a hefty tang. Both of the sturdy cutting edges are beautifully preserved and this remarkable weapon could be used with devastating results even today.[2] The importance of this example is further enhanced by the presence of a splendid pattern-welded iron inlaid inscription which is 12.5 cm long. It is possible to decipher almost all of the letters. However, a radiographic study of this sword carried out in the British Museum Research Laboratory revealed the inscription to be **+LEUTLRLL** with the final T inverted as below.[3] The inlay is pattern-welded and appears intact except for a tiny missing portion of the R. It is possible to see the simple but effective way in which the cross and letters are constructed. All of the inscription lies within the boundaries of the fuller. On the reverse side of the blade and centred at a distance of 9 cm from the crossguard is an iron-inlaid 'reversed S', thus **2**. Again, the inlay is pattern-welded.

Both lateral faces of the chunky curved crossguard carry copper-alloy decoration in the form of a series of diamond-shaped islands set in a sea of applied silver, which must have made this weapon staggeringly beautiful in its youth.[4] Under magnification, it is possible to see the fine parallel cuts onto which the silver and copper-alloy sheets were hammered. The upper hilt is composed of two pieces and rivet heads can be seen under the upper guard, which is a smaller similarly shaped version of the crossguard which also carries identical decoration. The trilobed pommel still retains some of the same type of decoration, especially on one side of the larger central lobe. This is in the form of an almost complete larger diamond. There is a deep and wide groove between the pommel and upper guard and grooves between the lobes of the pommel and these grooves, which are about 0.3 cm wide, almost certainly would have contained strips of silver. There are also traces of silver on the grip side of the crossguard.

continued →

→ Full length view of 1848, 10-21 1. Photograph courtesy of and copyright British Museum.

77

← continuation of British Museum, 1848, 10-21 1

It is worth noting that which Ewart Oakeshott wrote after handling this beautiful weapon: 'As your fingers close round its hilt you feel the character of the weapon; it seems positively to woo you to strike. There is no mistaking its message or purpose, even after an immersion in mud and water and weeds of eight or so centuries.'[5]

Evison noted two other sword blades with the same, or almost identical, inscriptions–one from Estonia, another from Russia and a possible third Anglo-Saxon copy from the Thames at Battersea.[6] The example from Russia was found at Almetyevo, but here the first T is inverted and the next letter is an inverted L. The central device upon the reverse side of this blade may well be the remains of an interlace pattern similar to those characteristically found on Ulfberht blades.[7]

[1] See Herbert Maryon, 'A Sword of the Viking Period from the River Witham', *The Antiquarian Journal* 30 (July to October, 1950), pp. 175–179.
[2] I first handled this sword in 1987 when Leslie Webster of the British Museum was delivering it to the William the Conqueror Exhibition in Rouen. I have never forgotten the experience.
[3] See the splendid contribution of Janet Lang and Barry Ager, 'Swords of the Anglo-Saxon and Viking Periods in the British Museum: a Radiographic Study', *Weapons and Warfare in Anglo-Saxon England*, ed. Sonia Chadwick Hawkes (Oxford, 1989), pp. 103–105.
[4] Much of the silver remains.
[5] See Ewart Oakeshott, *Records of the Medieval Sword* (Woodbridge, 1991), p. 26. See also Ian Peirce, 'The Development of the Medieval Sword, c. 850–1300', *Ideals and Practice of Medieval Knighthood: Papers from the Third Strawberry Hill Conference (1988)*, ed. C. Harper-Bill and Ruth Harvey, pp. 144–145.
[6] V.I. Evison, 'A Sword from the Thames at Wallingford Bridge', *Antiquarian Journal* 124 (1967), pp.160–189.
[7] A.N. Kirpichnikov, 'Drevnerusskoye oruzhiye (vyp. I) Mechi i Sabli, IX–XIII vv', *Arkheologiya SSR* (1966), E1–36, pl. XVII no. 4 and pl. XIX, no. 1–2.

→ Hilt of 1848, 10-21 1 showing strongly curved guards with copper alloy diamonds against a background of silver. Photograph courtesy of and copyright British Museum.

↓ Detail of iron inlay on blade of 1848, 10-21 1. Photograph courtesy of and copyright British Museum.

79

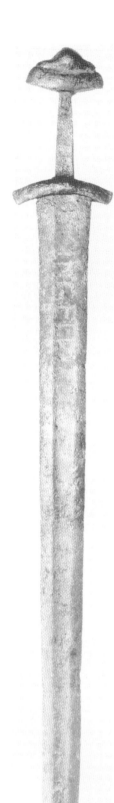

British Museum
1856, 7-1 1404

Date: late tenth to early eleventh century
Find-place: River Thames in King's Reach off the Temple in London, England
Overall length: 84.2 cm *Blade length:* 69.7 cm
Length of cross: 10.2 cm *Length of grip:* 8.5 cm
Balance point: 16.2 cm
Condition: excellent condition for a river find

This sword was found in the River Thames, in King's Reach, off the Temple in London. It was acquired by the British Museum in 1856 by purchase from Mr. Charles Roach Smith.

The beautifully complete and acutely tapered blade has a width of 5.7 cm at the crossguard and the point remains perfectly preserved. Both cutting edges are in a healthy state and bear many battle-nicks along their lengths. Some areas of the blade appear to boast their original surface whereas other portions are covered with a blackish patina.[1] The tapered fullers, 2.2 cm wide at their origin adjacent to the crossguard, run to within some 9 cm of the point. On one side and stretching more than the width of the fullers is a splendid **INGELRII** inscription, with all of the letters picked out in intricate pattern-welded iron inlay of a similar style to many of those illustrated by Leppäaho.[2] All of the inlay is intact and the inscription has a length of 11.7 cm. Upon the reverse side is another portion of inlay, again all intact, namely a cross potent flanked by three vertical bars. Leppäaho illustrated a sword which bears a cross potent between two omegas flanked by three vertical bars.[3] The tang of the sword is slightly tapered and appears to have been never robust.

The boat-shaped crossguard curves gracefully towards the blade and is better preserved on the side of the Ingelrii inscription, indeed still retaining some small traces of silver plating.[4] The upper guard is a smaller version of the cross and upon it is mounted a trilobate pommel consisting of a bulbous central lobe flanked by two tiny elongated ones. Small pieces of silver still cling to the surface of the pommel. Under magnification it can be seen that the decoration had been applied using the common technique of hatching the surface with an array of fine incisions and hammering on the sheets of precious metal. No rivets are in evidence, leading me to believe that the upper hilt was made in one piece. This is a sword which has graced many volumes, not least because of its stunning proportions.[5]

[1] The mud of the Thames, like many European rivers such as the Seine, the Danube and the Scheldt for example, seems to nurture any metallic object which it receives. It appears that the chemical content of the mud initially causes a reaction with the metal surface producing a substance called goethite $(FeO(OH))$ which protects against further corrosion.
[2] See, in particular, Jorma Leppäaho, *Späteisenzeitliche Waffen aus Finnland: Schwertinschriften und Waffenverzierungen des 9.–12. Jahrhunderts* (Helsinki, 1964), pp. 7, 9, 11, 37, 41, 43 and 47 for good examples.
[3] See Leppäaho, p. 25.
[4] I noticed this in November 2000 when I closely inspected the sword. I do not think this has been recorded before.
[5] See in particular Ewart Oakeshott, *Records of the Medieval Sword* (Woodbridge, 1991), p. 26; R. Ewart Oakeshott, *The Archaeology of Weapons* (London, 1960), pl. 6a; and Ian Peirce, 'The Development of the Medieval Sword, c. 850–1300', *Ideals and Practice of Medieval Knighthood: Papers from the Third Strawberry Hill Conference (1988)*, ed. C. Harper-Bill and Ruth Harvey, pp. 145–146 and pl. 4.

← ↑ Full length view and hilt detail of 1856, 7-1 1404 with wide oppositely curved guards. Photographs courtesy of and copyright British Museum.

↓ Details of 1856, 7-1 1404 showing the iron inlaid INGELRII inscription above and geometric inlay of **III✠III** on the opposite blade face on blade below. Photographs courtesy of and copyright British Museum.

1936:3763

Date: first half of the tenth century
Find-place: Wheelam, County Kildare, Ireland, 1936
Overall length: 93.7 cm *Blade length:* 81.5 cm
Length of cross: 12.2 cm *Length of grip:* 8.5 cm
Balance point: 15.0 cm
Condition: Both hilt and blade are in a fair state of preservation. The blade is corroded completely through in places corresponding to the position of the fullers.

This sword was found in a drain in marshy land and almost certainly not in its original place of deposition. It was cleaned and treated in the Research Laboratory in the British Museum, on behalf of the National Museum of Ireland and has a glossy black appearance.[1]

Although the blade is heavily corroded, it is still possible to detect the extremities of both fullers and cutting edges. The point of balance would have been even closer to the hilt if the upper element of the pommel were in place. Also, the great width of the blade at the cross (6.0 cm) encourages the weapon to be well balanced in the hand.

On one side of the blade, at a distance of 11.0 cm, from the hilt, are the remains of an iron-inlaid inscription, in the form of a Lombardic letter 'O'.

The cross curves gently towards the blade, is elliptical in cross-section with rounded ends and has straight, lateral sides.

The lower element of the pommel is smaller than the cross, but has the same cross-sectional shape. The upper part of the pommel is missing, but traces of the iron rivets by which it had been attached are evident. The tang is broad and robust. There is no sign of any decoration upon the hilt.

This weapon reminds me so much of the great Viking sword found in the River Witham near Lincoln and now in the British Museum.[2] It has a trilobed pommel and is described in detail elsewhere (see pp. 77–79). I believe this Irish example is of exactly the same hilt and blade type as that superb example in the British Museum.[3]

[1] See Johs. Bøe, 'Norse Antiquities in Ireland', *Viking Antiquities in Great Britain and Ireland, Part III*, ed. Haakon Shetelig (Oslo, 1940), p. 85 and fig. 54, p. 82.
[2] Accession number 1848, 10-21 1; described and illustrated herein on pp. 77–79.
[3] See also Jan Petersen, *De Norske Vikingesverd* (Oslo, 1919), p. 124 and fig. 102 and the splendid example from Universitetets Oldsaksamling, Museum No. C4397 (pp. 92–93 herein) found in a male grave with other weapons, tools, and horse equipment, illustrated in *From Viking to Crusader: The Scandinavians and Europe 800 to 1200* (22nd Council of Europe Exhibition) (Copenhagen, 1992), p. 255, cat. no. 110. That sword, however, is a Petersen type P.

← Full length view of 1936:3763. Corrosion has pierced the blade in multiple places along the fullers. Photograph courtesy of and copyright National Museum of Ireland.

→ View of the hilt of 1936:3763. No evidence of any applied decoration remains. If not for the evidence of the rivets, and thus the former presence of a pommel, this would more closely fit Petersen's type Q. Photograph courtesy of and copyright National Museum of Ireland.

83

J3

Date: mid ninth to mid tenth century
Overall length: 90.0 cm *Blade length:* 75.0 cm
Length of cross: 10.0 cm *Length of grip:* 12.0 cm
Condition: excellent

The blade of this beautifully proportioned weapon is in excellent condition as indeed is the hilt. It is almost certainly a river-find, but the museum records tell us no more than, 'it was put into the museum by Benjamin Fillon, a Vendeen archaeologist, who died around 1890'. It dates from c. 850 to before 950. Petersen dated this type accurately from 'find combinations', i.e. the types of spears and axes found with a sword.

The blade is some 5.3 cm wide at the hilt and has not been subjected to any cleaning process. The well-defined fullers occupy about half the width of the blade and run down to within a few centimetres of the point. This is one of those rare blades where the point is perfectly preserved.[1]

The cutting edges, which show much evidence of honing (and thus pointing to a well-used weapon), are in such excellent condition that this sword could be used, quite literally, even today.

Many swords have lost the top element of their pommel and it would be very easy to assign this weapon to that category. There is, however, no evidence that this specimen ever had a top hamper to its pommel. Jan Petersen recognized this as a unique type in its own right and called it a type M.[2]

The long cross is roughly rectangular in cross-section with slightly rounded extremities, and the tiny bar-like pommel tapers gently towards each end.

It is characteristic of this type that the fullers are wide and deep, thus lightening the blade considerably (without impairing its strength) and therefore making it unnecessary to have an overly massive pommel to counteract the mass of the blade.

The example under discussion should be compared with the equally well-preserved type M (c. 900) from Mogen, Rauland, Telemark, found in a male grave along with a splendid long-bladed and decorated spear, an arrowhead and a pin.[3]

This type, apart from type H, is the most common form of the Viking Age and according to Petersen one of the simplest. He was aware of a total of 198 specimens found in Norway. Of these, 166 had double-edged blades, 30 had single-edged blades and two were in such condition that their status in this regard could not be determined. They came mostly from the eastern part of Norway, none had inscriptions and two were pattern-welded.

Type 'M' first appeared in the middle of the ninth century, becoming more common in the second half of that century and most likely continuing into the first few decades of the tenth century. There are sub-types of type M, based upon slightly curved crosses and pommel bars.

[1] As one would expect, the last 3.0 cm or so of a blade would be highly stressed when slashing or thrusting.
[2] See Jan Petersen, *De Norske Vikingesverd* (Oslo, 1919), pp. 117–125 and figs. 98 and 99, the swords from Ovri Eidsvold and Romerike, respectively.

footnotes continue on p. 86 →

Hilt of J3 showing straight, unadorned guards and the absence of a pommel, characteristic of Petersen's type M. Photograph courtesy of and copyright by the Musée de l'Armée, Paris, negative K23711.

Full length view of J3. Photograph courtesy of and copyright by the Musée de l'Armée, Paris, negative K23710.

Recorded as no. 78 in the early records and as C24244 in the modern records at The University of Oslo, Institute for Archaeology. The blade of this grave find is some 10.0 cm (4.0″) larger than the Paris example and the blade side of the cross has a 'peculiar ornamentation consisting of deeply branded (drilled) points (holes)'.

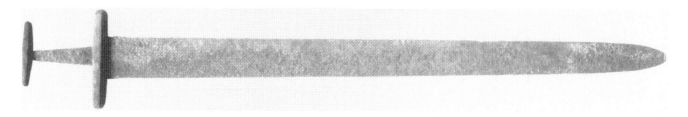

↑ C24244 from Mogen, Rauland, Telemark, Norway. Photograph courtesy of and copyright Universitetets Oldsaksamling.

↓ Shortened sword with a diminutive type M hilt which appears to have been made from a full sized Viking sword, with the present sword blade representing the forte. Reputedly from a boy's grave in Ringebu, Oppland, Norway opened in the late 19th century and found with a similarly small axe head, spear head and shield boss. Overall length: 47.7 cm; blade length: 38.5 cm; maximum blade thickness: 0.48 cm; weight 409 g. Private collection. Photograph by Doug Whitman.

Petersen type N

Type N was characterized by Peterson as having an unadorned rounded pommel upon a straight upper guard. In a series of seven examples examined by Petersen, pommels were between 2.4 and 3.0 cm in height. Upper guards ranged between 7.2 and 8.3 cm with thicknesses of just over 1 cm, while the crossguards averaged 10 cm in length with a late example reaching a maximum of 15.4 cm. Blades are generally double-edged.

Peterson was uncertain as to whether this was an independent type or represented a simplification of earlier trilobate pommels. Petersen dated this type to the second half of the 9th century.

→ C4115 in the Universitetets Oldsaksamling, Oslo, captioned Fig. 103. Nordby, Fet, Akh., from Jan Petersen, *De Norske Vikingesverd* (Oslo, 1919), pp. 125–126.

C13848a

Date: first half of the tenth century
Find-place: Vestre Berg, Løiten parish, Akershus, Norway
Overall length: 95.8 cm   *Blade length:* 79.5 cm
Length of cross: 10.7 cm   *Length of grip:* 10.9 cm
Condition: hilt very good, blade badly corroded

This 'ritually killed' late ninth to tenth century sword is part of a very large grave find from Vestre Berg, in the parish of Løiten, in Akershus county. According to the museum register, the grave was discovered by 'clearing wood, between some rocks'. Other artifacts recovered from the grave were, a sword (very small), two arrows, one axe head, two shield bosses, one sax and a massive assortment of other iron objects including hooks, a lock for a chest, and a horse bit.[1] Several of the artifacts had *glødeskall* and all were quite well preserved.

continued →

↓ View of C13848a showing how the sword has been bent. The bowl from another Viking Age find is C9529. Photograph courtesy of and copyright Universitetets Oldsaksamling, negative 15653a.

← continuation of Universitetets Oldsaksamling, C13848a

The blade is complete and has been ritually bent, into a rather graceful 'S' shape.[2] It is badly pitted overall, with at least three small holes towards the point, and it may well be pattern-welded. The tang is broad, sturdy, and long, as befits such a fine blade.

The hilt is the result of fine craftsmanship. The boat-shaped cross has rounded ends and curves gracefully towards the blade, a point which Petersen emphasises as being a characteristic of a genuine type O. At one time, it and the beautifully fashioned five lobed pommel were completely covered in a very light coloured bronze coating.[3] Now only traces are in evidence but sufficient to formulate an image of the appearance of this hilt at the time of its creation or soon after. The cross carries three deeply inscribed decorative panels on each lateral face, and this form of decoration may well have had considerable significance during the period of the ninth and tenth centuries. The superb pommel has retained rather more of its bronze coating than the cross. The upper guard is almost identical in shape to the cross, but curves very gently away from the blade, completing a geometrically harmonic bond between all parts of the hilt. Each lateral face bears three decorative panels almost identical to those on the cross. The pommel consists of five lobes, all quite beautifully wrought. The three larger, and central, ones have similar decorative devices to those on the cross (and on both lateral faces) whereas the splayed, tilting outer elements carry no form of decoration. There is no evidence of rivets holding the upper guard and pommel together and it may well be that a braising technique was used. This is a beautifully formed hilt and it does appear that both the cross and pommel were manufactured by a casting process.[4] Indeed, a number of cast bronze hilt elements with similar knot-like ornamentation have been described.[5]

Fig. 105. Gunnarsby, Rygge, Smaal. ½.

Petersen includes this weapon in his group I in which there are eleven other swords, all with double-edged blades, as far as these are identifiable. He also was of the opinion that 'two to three detached guards of bronze' also belong to the same group.[6] Group II of this type have hilts 'covered in silver plate' and group III have significantly less high lobes and the decoration consists of plain, inlaid strips.

[1] The axe is a type E according to Jan Petersen, *De Norske Vikingesverd* (Oslo, 1919), p. 131.
[2] Petersen also records the presence of a rattle, and a double oval bronze buckle with this find.
[3] Petersen refers to the lobes as tongues, and quite appropriately.
[4] Most certainly, the uniformity of all parts of the hilt leads me to believe that they were indeed cast the bronze coating then applied by a planishing, hammering process.
[5] See Alfred Geibig, *Beiträge zur morphologischen Entwicklung des Schwertes im Mittelalter: Eine Analyse des Fundmaterials vom ausgehenden 8. bis zum 12. Jahrhundert aus Sammlungen der Bundesrepublik Deutschland* (Neumünster, 1991), cat. no. 317 (table 161, #8) for a crossguard and cat. no. 274 (table 155, #4) for an upper guard found in Haddebyer Noor, accession 13018 in the Wikinger Museum Haithabu. Lee Jones further discusses these and still another example of such a crossguard mounted on an earlier blade at www.vikingsword.com/vmuseum/vmo1.html (30 January 1999).
[6] Petersen, p. 127.

← Figure 105 from Jan Petersen, *De Norske Vikingesverd* (Oslo, 1919), p. 128 showing the hilt of a sword, C16380 in the collection of the Universitetets Oldsaksamling, from Gunnarsby, Rygge, Smaal. at 1/2 of actual size.

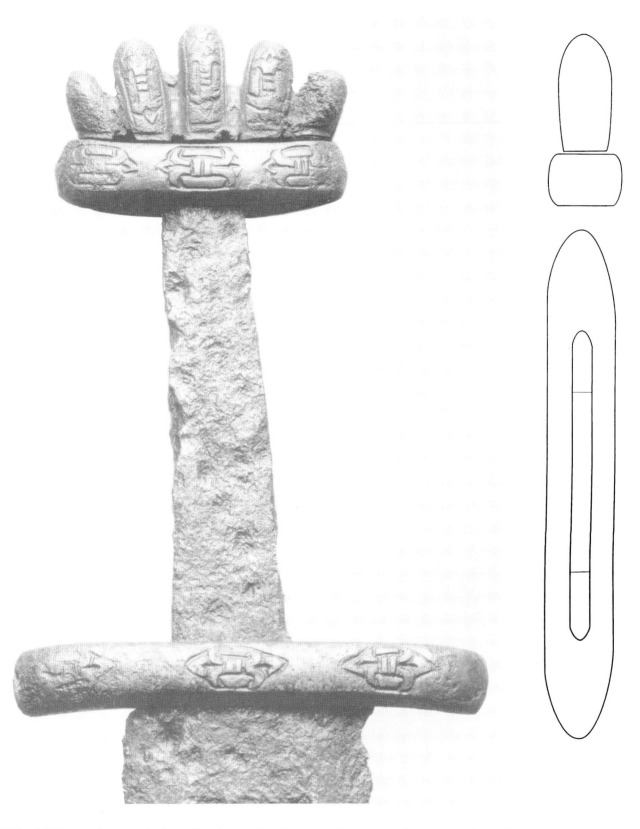

↑ Hilt of C13848a showing the knot-like decoration. Photograph courtesy of and copyright by the Universitetets Oldsaksamling, negative 23352/13.

↗ The outlines of the pommel from the side and of the crossguard from below are adapted from fig. 104 of Jan Petersen, *De Norske Vikingesverd* (Oslo, 1919), p. 127, which is an illustration of this hilt.

Date: tenth century
Find-place: River Thames at Kew, England
Overall length: 75.3 cm *Blade length:* 63 cm
Length of cross: 12.8 cm *Length of grip:* 9.5 cm
Condition: hilt good; blade mostly heavily corroded

This sword was found in the Thames at Kew and donated to the British Museum by Sir A. W. Franks. It probably dates from the tenth century, but this type was popular well into the later Viking Age.

The blade is heavily corroded, although the last seven to eight centimetres is beautifully preserved, as indeed is the extreme tip.[1] On one side of the blade large amounts of scabbard material are adhering, but it is still possible to make out the contours of a fuller. The blade tapers elegantly and this feature, combined with the wide fuller and extremely short blade, being just under 25 inches, would have given the sword a fine balance.[2] It was not possible to detect any inlaid inscription with the human eye, due to the corrosion and the mass of organic material sticking to the blade. However, a radiographic study carried out by the British Museum revealed the existence of a double-sided inscription with resulting superimposition of inlaid iron letters on the x-ray plate image.[3] The interpretation remains purely tentative, being **INGELRII** on one side and **SITAN(B)I** or conversely **I(B)NATIS** on the opposite.[4] Clearly, the superimposition of the inscriptions from both sides over one another does make it difficult to define the letters and easy to see what is not there. The sophisticated techniques of the B.A.M. in Berlin could surely solve the problem and give a positive identity to both of the inscriptions.[5]

The elegant canoe-shaped crossguard curves gracefully towards the blade. It still bears large quantities of applied latten sheet upon its lateral faces, this having been hammered onto a surface prepared with an array of incised crosshatched cuts. Again, a large amount of this superb decoration has survived on the grip side of the crossguard, but not on the blade side. The upper guard is a smaller but almost identical version of the crossguard and also bears a similar decoration on the lateral faces. The missing pommel was riveted to the upper guard, and the latter still carries a hole on one side and the remains of a rivet on the other.

[1] It is always a rarity for the tip to have survived under such circumstances due to the thinness of the metal at that point.
[2] All of the above-mentioned features would have driven the centre of gravity close to the cross, a much-desired quality.
[3] Double-sided inscriptions of inlaid iron cause great difficulties in interpretation due to the superimposition of the letters upon the x-ray plates and low contrast against the background blade metal. Double-sided inscriptions inlaid with thin silver wire stand out in much greater contrast from the fabric of the blade and are therefore much, much easier to interpret, especially using stereoradiography. See Jorma Leppäaho, *Späteisenzeitliche Waffen aus Finnland: Schwertinschriften und Waffenverzierungen des 9.–12. Jahrhunderts* (Helsinki, 1964), fig. 27, 1c and 1d, p. 59.
[4] Janet Lang and Barry Ager, 'Swords of the Anglo-Saxon and Viking Periods in the British Museum: a Radiographic Study', *Weapons and Warfare in Anglo-Saxon England*, ed. Sonia Chadwick Hawkes (Oxford, 1989), p. 106 and fig. 7.9c, p. 102.
[5] The work of the B.A.M. is known as being in the van of non-destructive analysis of artifacts.

← Full length view of 1891, 9-5 3. Photograph courtesy of and copyright British Museum.

→ Hilt of 1891, 9-5 3. The pommel is presently missing, but evidence of its former attachment remains. Photograph courtesy of and copyright British Museum.

91

C4397

Date: first half of the tenth century
Find-place: Svere Farm, Lier, Buskeruds, Norway
Overall length: 86.8 cm *Blade length:* 74.6 cm
Length of cross: 11.1 cm *Length of grip:* 8.7 cm
Condition: hilt excellent; blade pitted, but usable even today

This sword was found in 1868 in a grave mound on the Farm of Svere in the area called Lier in Buskeruds. It was found with a spear head, an axe head, a shield, a file, a curved tool, the bit of a bridle, a sickle blade, a hook, and the fragmented pieces of a kettle. The museum register also states, 'Several of the pieces found are works of unusual beauty, specifically the curved tool … and the sword.' It dates from the first half of the tenth century.

The blade is complete and still extremely sound even with the heavy surface pitting in most areas. It is as straight and true as the day its maker completed it. The cutting edges and fullers are quite discernible. Unusually, the fuller on one side is not centrally placed for the first 15 cm from the cross,[1] the cutting edge on one side being 2 cm wide and barely 1.5 cm upon the other.[2] Again, unusually, the tip is completely preserved, which is somewhat of a rarity.[3] The tang is huge and sturdy, thus imparting much added strength to the union of the hilt and blade. It is nicely tapered in both width and thickness, the work of a great craftsman, with a strong arm and a steady eye.

It is the copper and silver decorations on the lateral faces of the crossguard and upper guard (the pommel is lost) which announce the considerable importance of this outstanding jewel of war.[4] The boat-shaped cross is gracefully curved towards the blade and the similarly shaped upper guard (except for a small pointed feature at the upper central region) curves away from the blade. Both guards are slightly splayed at the ends.[5] The decoration is mostly made up of three strands of plaited silver wire bounded by single strands of copper wire, and all parallel to the blade.[6] Occasionally, one can see in a few isolated places where plaited copper has been used, probably the result of a repair. The overall effect is strikingly beautiful and the result of many hours of precise and delicate workmanship.

[1] Not illustrated.
[2] Most certainly *not* due to corrosion, but probably due to the tool misalignment during manufacture.
[3] The blade tip being the thinnest part of the blade and thus usually first distorted by corrosion.
[4] The museum register is incorrect. It states that the weapon is 'decorated very nicely with embedded silver on both guards'. The decoration is of silver and copper. See *From Viking to Crusader: The Scandinavians and Europe 800 to 1200* (22nd Council of Europe Exhibition) (Copenhagen, 1992), cat. no. 110, p. 255.
[5] See Jan Petersen, *De Norske Vikingesverd* (Oslo, 1919), pp. 134–135, fig. 109.
[6] I actually made up a sample of plaited wires in my workshop to ensure my statement was correct.

← Full length view of C4397. Photograph by Ove Holst courtesy of and copyright Universitetets Oldsaksamling, negative 21643.

→ Hilt of C4397 showing the applied silver and copper herring-bone pattern. Photograph by Eirik Irgens Johnsen courtesy of and copyright Universitetets Oldsaksamling, negative 23352/ 15.

93

C19763

Date: tenth century
Find-place: Kjørven farm, Lunner parish, Jevnaker, Norway
Overall length: 91.5 cm *Blade length:* 79.3 cm
Length of cross: 11 cm *Length of grip:* 9.5 cm
Balance point: 21.2 cm
Condition: good, in some places excellent due to *glødeskall*; the hilt is heavily corroded, but complete

This tenth century sword was found in a grave mound at Kjørven farm in the parish of Lunner, Jevnaker. Close to the mound, another similar weapon was found which also had *glødeskall*. [1]

The cutting edges are well formed and beautifully preserved except for the last 26 cm. They also show much evidence of use, there being a number of deep nicks, especially towards the point.[2] The fullers have also been blessed with the retention of their shape and form, for most of their length. The areas of *glødeskall* are close to the hilt and in the central portion of the blade area and here the surface is almost pristine, with no trace of pitting. The tapered tang is huge and strong

The simply shaped Indian canoe type of cross is badly corroded, but intact and has a gentle curve towards the blade. The upper guard is smaller, similarly shaped, with blunted ends and curves in the opposite direction. The hilt of this sword is quite plain, with no trace of any decoration, and is of the same profile as the silver and copper decorated one found in a grave mound on the farm of Svere (C4397, see pp. 92–93 herein).

Petersen lists 122 of this type of which 118 blades are double-edged.[3] The other weapon, which was found close by, must have had a two-piece pommel because the upper guard still has rivets in place. It also had *glødeskall* at several sites along the blade.

[1] The accession number of this weapon found close by is C19763-64.
[2] A much-used blade also needed to be regularly honed, which is the case with this weapon.
[3] Jan Petersen, *De Norske Vikingesverd* (Oslo, 1919), pp. 136–140.

← Full length view of C19763. Photograph by Ove Holst courtesy of and copyright Universitetets Oldsaksamling, negative 19188.

↓ Closeup of the blade of C19763 showing the *glødeskall*. Photograph by Ian Peirce.

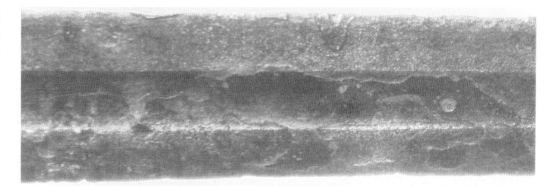

1864, 1-27 3

Date: tenth century
Find-place: Lough Gur, near Grange, near Holycross, Co. Limerick, Ireland
Overall length: 76.3 cm *Blade length:* 66.6 cm
Length of cross: 7.7 cm *Length of grip:* 6.8 cm
Balance point: 14.6 cm
Condition: excellent for most of the blade length

This is a tiny little sword and I was unable to hold it properly due to the shortness of the grip. The British Museum register of swords tells us it was found at Lough Gur, near Grange, near Holycross, Co. Limerick, Ireland and donated by J.F.W. de Salis.[1]

Both the fullers and the cutting edges are in a fine state of preservation for some two-thirds of their length, but unfortunately the last third of the blade is badly corroded. Both sides of the blade bear pattern-welded inlaid decoration. Upon one side there are three vertical bars followed by a cross potent, a central circle, a cross potent and finally another set of three vertical bars. Almost all of the inlay is intact: III✚O✚III. Upon the reverse side there is a group of three vertical bars followed by an omega-like device, a cross potent, another omega with some inlay missing and finally three more vertical bars, also with missing inlay: IIIC✚ƆIII.

Leppäaho illustrates a pommel-less sword from Lempäälä which has Ɔ8✚8Ɔ on one side of the blade. Again, the sword from Loppi has almost identical inscriptions to the one under consideration. On one side IIIC✚ƆIII and upon the other III✚ O ✚III. Note that only the cross flanked by the omegas is a cross potent. Finally from Leppäaho, the so important fragment of the blade found at Sääksmäki with the most splendidly preserved inscriptions, shown on p. 8. On one side ✚VLFBERH✚ and on the reverse side IIIC✚ƆIII and almost identical to the Lough Gur example.[2] Lorange also, as you would expect, knew of sword blades bearing intriguing devices. One such grave find from Thorblaa, Hardanger, found in 1871, bore some elements also seen on the British Museum example. Namely O✚O, which may or may not be flanked by groups of vertical bars.[3]

The tiny canoe-shaped crossguard curves gently towards the blade and bears no form of decoration. Adhering to it on the grip side is an oval brass ferrule with decorative fluting. The unusual little upper guard is a smaller version of the crossguard and has a similar decorated brass ferrule sticking to its underside.

This is a prestige weapon and Hilda Davidson may well be correct when she alludes to this being the sword of a high-born boy.

[1] The register also states 'lakebed', so we must presume it was literally found in the lake. Hilda Ellis Davidson states that it came from a crannog.
[2] Jorma Leppäaho, *Späteisenzeitliche Waffen aus Finnland: Schwertinschriften und Waffenverzierungen des 9.–12. Jahrhunderts* (Helsinki, 1964), sword NM 4254, pl. 9, no. 4 on pp. 22–23; sword NM 2345:1, pl. 10, no. 1 on pp. 24–25 (the inscription is pattern-welded) and sword NM 2767, pl. 16, no. b on pp. 36–37 (the inscription is also pattern-welded). Lee Jones and I had the good fortune to study this splendid example in Helsinki.
[3] A.L. Lorange, *Den Yngre Jernalders Sværd* (Bergen, 1889), tab. III, 5.

→ Full length view of 1864, 1-27 3. Photograph courtesy of and copyright British Museum.

C257

Date: tenth century
Find-place: Hedemarken, Norway
Overall length presently: 77.1 cm *Estimated original length:* 85 cm *Blade length:* 63 cm
Length of cross: 10.7 cm *Length of grip:* 9.2 cm
Condition: some areas of blade are in excellent condition, as indeed are all elements
of the hilt

According to the register, this tenth century sword was 'found in the earth in Hedemarken'.[1] It was cleaned in 1887 when more of the copper interlace decoration was found. According to the telltale remaining parts, this blade was never wide, neither was it overly long; I estimate 70 cm original length, at the most. It is badly corroded in two places down its length and some 7 or 8 cm of the tip is missing. There is hardly any discernible evidence of the blade being sharpened and the cutting edges are proud and well defined.[2] On one side of the blade much of the original surface survives, stretching for a distance of 25 cm from the cross and within the deep, broad fuller is a beautifully executed **+ULFBERHT+** iron inlaid inscription, fully 19.5 cm in length. An entry in the register, under the year 1887, records the inscription as **VLVBERN**, but Petersen clearly read it as **+ULFBERHT+**, as indeed I did in 1993 and again in 1998. Upon the reverse side of the blade, it is still possible to make out the typical decoration associated with any Ulfberht blade,[3] although some of the inlay is missing.

The boat-like crossguard is flared at the ends and both lateral faces are entirely covered with embedded, scrolled and spiralling interlace, picked out in copper. Inside of the copper lanes is further decoration with applied silver and the eye-catching effect is further enhanced by a series of small punch holes every millimetre or so. The pommel and upper guard are decorated in a similar manner, and while the upper guard is smaller than the crossguard, it is identical in shape. The five-lobed pommel has a bulbous central element flanked by two equally bulbous, but smaller ones, the latter two attached to a pair of outer lobes not unlike a raised and basking tortoise head.[4] Almost as if to complete the decorations upon the cake, as it were, four tiny bridges, in the shape of flattened monkey nuts and made of bright bronze, span the space between the central and sandwiched lobes. This is in itself an almost unique and highly refined finishing touch to the hilt of this great sword. There is also sufficient evidence to suggest that the 0.3 cm wide grooves between each lobe may well have once held some form of decorative strip.

Lorange illustrates a sword which has an almost identical hilt to the one presently under consideration. It was found at Vad i Etme Søndhordland and is museum no. 961.[5] The decoration on the guards of that sword is identical. We even have the little tortoise-like heads flanking the central part of the pommel. The little flattened monkey nut bridges are also in place and the blade carries an Ulfberht inscription. There can be little doubt that these two great weapons came from the same workshop and what a remarkable group of craftsmen must have toiled within its walls. A wonderful blade, a superbly fashioned hilt, even if it were plain, outstanding hilt decoration and a fine Ulfberht inscription! Even without the tip of the blade, there is a touching harmony between blade and hilt. How much more glorious would it have looked a thousand years ago? You will all understand my feelings when handling this great weapon. It is not surprising that Jan Petersen featured this intriguing sword in his splendid book.

← Full length view of C257.
Photograph by Ove Holst
courtesy of and copyright
Universitetets Oldsaksamling,
negative 22344D.

→ Hilt of C257. Photograph
courtesy of and copyright
Universitetets Oldsaksamling,
negative 3513.

[1] Jan Petersen, *De Norske Vikingesverd* (Oslo, 1919), p. 141, fig. 113.
[2] Although the cutting edges do not bear traces of much honing, there are plenty of nicks in evidence indicating this to be a well-used weapon.
[3] Both Lee Jones and I made the same reading in 1993.
[4] My wife and I have kept and adored tortoises for many years and I was struck by the likeness of these outer lobes to the attitude of a tortoise enjoying the sun.
[5] See A.L. Lorange, *Den Yngre Jernalders Sværd* (Bergen, 1889), tab. I, fig. 1, for this other Ulfberht with identical decorations on the cross. See also the sword from Brekke, Vik i Sogn in Lorange, tab. III, fig. 8, which is also an Ulfberht.

Date: tenth century
Find-place: Mixnam's Pit, Chertsey, England
Overall length: 98.4 cm *Blade length:* 81 cm
Length of cross: 13.3 cm *Length of grip:* 9.5 cm
Balance point: 12.7 cm
Condition: blade excellent but has a small gentle curve to it; hilt is complete with traces of decoration

It was a source of great joy to view and handle one of the very best Viking Age swords to have been found in England. The River Witham sword in the British Museum may well be viewed as the best, but this Chertsey sword of type S, for different reasons, could be its equal.[1] It was found in 1981 by Harry Cooper, an employee of the gravel company A. & J. Bull, Ltd., while extracting gravel by machine from the quarries known as Mixnam's Pit.

The long tapered blade is in very good condition with some areas of its surface in almost mint condition. The fullers and cutting edges are still well defined. On one side and set within the confines of the shallow fuller is a fine iron inlaid Ulfberht inscription characteristically placed between two crosses.[2] The inscription actually reads **+MFBERIT+**. On the reverse side of the blade is a single cross and a typical Ulfberht design, that is, a lattice pattern set within two groups of three vertical bars.

The hilt is beautifully formed and is so similar to the big 780-4 in Copenhagen (see pp. 100–101). The boat shaped crossguard bears the remains of a splendid decoration on its lateral faces; all achieved with silver and copper inlays. From what remains of the inlay it appears that silver wire was wound round a copper wire and then hammered into place upon base metal which had been prepared with a scored surface to secure the overlay. The design was then bordered by fine copper wires. There is also a faint simple outline design on the upper surface of the crossguard. Also present are traces of similar decoration upon the flanking lobes of the pommel and upon the upper guard. Upon the robust tang and adjacent to the cross are traces of the grip and, although these have not been analysed, they do appear to be horn.

One other type S has been found in England, namely the great weapon probably found in the River Thames at the Temple Church. Its hilt is also decorated with an inlay of silver and copper-alloy in the Mammen style.[3]

[1] The River Witham sword and that from Chertsey are of different hilt styles. Both have decoration on their hilts, but it may well be that that on the Chertsey weapon was originally more splendid.
[2] A variant on the inscription is **+ULFBERH+T**, as can be seen in the Copenhagen weapon, accession 780-4, pp. 100–101 herein.
[3] *From Viking to Crusader: The Scandinavians and Europe 800 to 1200* (22nd Council of Europe Exhibition) (Copenhagen, 1992), cat. no. 413, p. 335. The sword from the Thames is in the British Museum, museum number M and LA 1887, 2-9 1.

← Full length view of CHYMS 2465. Photograph reproduced by courtesy of the Trustees of the British Museum.
→ Hilt of CHYMS 2465 showing the bulbous pommel and guards. Photograph reproduced by courtesy of the Trustees of the British Museum.

Date: tenth century
Overall length: 90.1 cm *Blade length:* 73.7 cm
Length of cross: 12.5 cm *Length of grip:* 8.8 cm
Balance point: 6.5 cm
Condition: excavated condition; hilt good with some vestiges of decoration remaining; blade overall well defined with some areas of deep pitting

This splendid tenth century weapon, whose reputation is further enhanced by an Ulfberht inscription, has an unusually finely, well tapered blade.[1] Both the fullers and cutting edges retain good definition with some areas in an excellent state of preservation. The blade may have been bent and imperfectly straightened. The inscription reads **+VLFBERH+T**, whereas normally the name is placed between the two crosses. This inscription is unusually close to the crossguard, which leads one to believe that the blade has been shortened and or rehilted in antiquity. Most of the iron inlay in the name has gone, although some remains, the **T** for example, but not so in the characteristic geometric pattern upon the reverse side of the blade where most remains intact. The general appearance of this example leads to the opinion that it is a river find, which would probably account for much of the missing inlay. It is a beautifully well-balanced weapon to handle and there is a striking resemblance between this weapon and the Chertsey sword, found in a gravel pit in 1981.[2] (See pp. 98–99 herein.)

Both the guards and the pommel are covered with a network of crosshatched cuts, indicating that at one time the whole surface of the entire hilt, aside from the grip, was plated with silver, of which only a few traces now remain in the grooves. The upper guard and the pommel are riveted together, which is commonly observed for this type and most others with two piece upper hilts. The face of the crossguard adjacent to the grip also shows traces of black tarnished silver.[3] In contrast, the Chertsey sword does not show evidence of having all of the hilt surfaces sheathed in silver, but rather has a pattern of somewhat spidery interlace, almost paper-chain-like in character.

Petersen lists some 22 of type S, which includes the sword under consideration. Two others among his Norwegian material also have Ulfberht inscriptions, namely C4690 from Aaker, Vang, Hedemarken and C571 from Nordgaarden, Sparbu, North Trondhjem.[4] Most interestingly two come from the same location (C237 and B1564) of Sandbu, Vaage, Kristians, as indeed do C7236 and C19754, both found at Hundstad, Hole, Buskered. To this list we may also add the fine Chertsey specimen, which also has a fine Ulfberht inscription. No two swords, of those which I have actually seen or of which I have seen photographs, appear to have similar decoration upon their hilts, but even so, some may well be the product of a single workshop.[5]

[1] Inspection of the blade shows that this is not due to regular honing, as the actual cutting edges, upon both sides of the blade, are almost intact. Such an acutely tapered Ulfberht is quite rare. Most of those that are well tapered are well-used swords which required the effectiveness of their cutting edges to be restored. See pp. 124–125. See also Jan Petersen, *De Norske Vikingesverd* (Oslo, 1919), pp. 142–149.
[2] See pp. 98–99 for the Chertsey sword, which retains more silver decoration than this Copenhagen example upon its hilt.

↑ Copenhagen 780-4 (upper) detail of crossguard and iron inlaid **+VLFBERH+T** inscription; (lower) detail of opposite site of hilt and the forte of the blade showing iron inlaid geometric patterns. Photographs courtesy of and copyright National Museum of Denmark.

← Copenhagen 780-4 full length view. Photograph courtesy of and copyright by the National Museum of Denmark

[3] See also Ian Peirce, 'The Development of the Medieval Sword, c. 850–1300', *Ideals and Practice of Medieval Knighthood: Papers from the Third Strawberry Hill Conference*, ed. C. Harper-Bill and Ruth Harvey (Woodbridge, 1988), p. 141 and plates 2a and 2b.
[4] Petersen, p. 143.
[5] See especially Petersen, figs. 114–116.

Date: tenth century
Find-place: Sandbu farm, Vaage, Oppland, Norway
Overall length presently: 53.5 cm *Blade length:* 36.1 cm
Length of cross: 12.8 cm *Length of grip:* 9.0 cm
Condition: hilt very good and complete; blade cutting edges still hold their shape, but are deeply pitted; fullers excellent, boasting some of their original surface

The museum register does not give much detail with regard to the finding of this exceptionally hilted tenth century weapon. It merely states 'grave find from the early Iron Age, from Sandbu farm in Vaage, Oppland'.

The blade may well have once been massively long on this weapon.[1] The very nature of the break at the end of the blade, and the bend preceding it, indicate that this sword was the victim of a ritual killing.

The hilt is Petersen type S, which according to the examples illustrated in his book, may be trilobated or have five lobes.[2] Both guards are of a similar boat-like shape with splayed ends and are formed of solid iron.[3] Their lateral faces were originally covered with silver plate, onto which intricate whirling interlaced patterns had been cut to reveal the iron base. Petersen records this pattern most beautifully in fig. 115 where it does appear that more of the silver was in place. Here and there are minute traces of copper. The upper and lower faces of the crossguard still retain small traces of this decoration, in comparison with swords from Aarhus and Vesterhang illustrated by Petersen, which appear to retain decoration of a geometric nature and much of it.[4] On the example under consideration, no traces of decoration have survived on the lower face of the upper guard.

The five lobed pommel is riveted to the upper guard, with the attachment holes still visible. Small traces of silver still cling to the surfaces. It is almost certain that the boundaries between each pommel lobe would have been filled with silver wire, in some form or another.[5]

The style of hilt decoration on the three type S swords illustrated by Petersen are all very different, as indeed it is upon the type S found while extracting gravel from Mixnam's pit and taken to Chertsey Museum (see 98–99 herein).

[1] The huge hilt would have almost demanded a long blade, especially as the width of the blade at the hilt is 6.2 cm. Sword 780-4 from Copenhagen has a blade length of 73.7 cm.
[2] See in particular, Jan Petersen, *De Norske Vikingesverd* (Oslo, 1919), figs. 114–116.
[3] Not all are solid. Many of the type S hilts, which I have handled, are hollow.
[4] Again, Petersen, figs. 114 and 116.
[5] Such as a thick strand of silver wire, twisted strands or even a beaded wire.

↗ Profile of the bulbous pommel and upper guard from the side (above) and to a smaller scale, the crossguard (below), adapted from Sofie Krafft's illustration of this sword, fig. 115, p. 144 in Petersen.

→ Hilt of C237. Photograph courtesy of and copyright Universitetets Oldsaksamling, negative 7423.

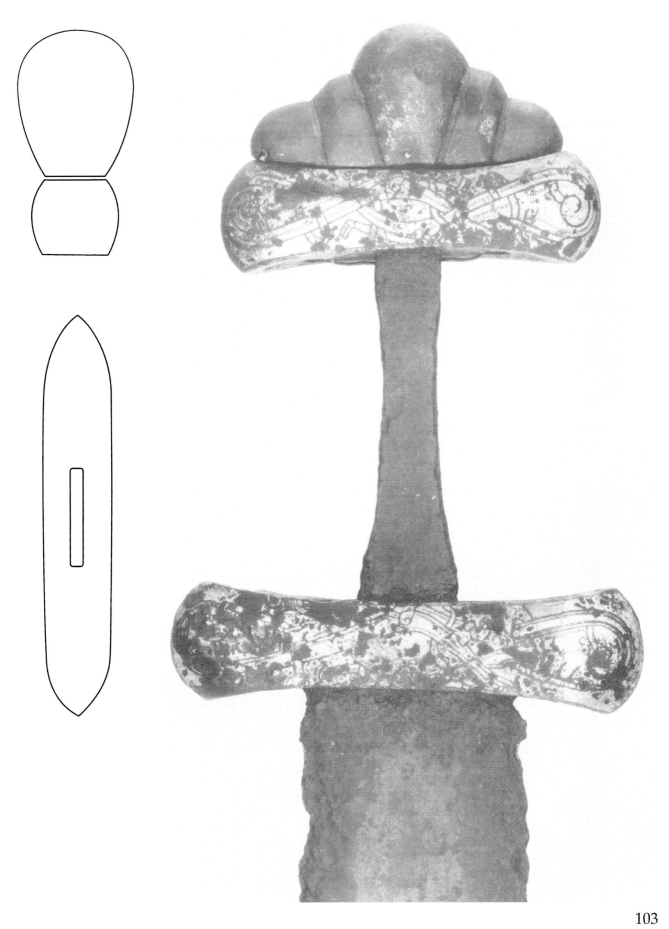

British Museum, London
1887, 2-9 1

Date: tenth century
Find-place: possibly River Thames at Temple Church, London, England
Overall length: 88.5 cm *Blade length:* 72.3 cm
Length of cross: 11.4 cm *Length of grip:* 8.6 cm
Balance point: 8 cm
Condition: hilt very good in places; blade heavily corroded

There appears to be no certainty with regard to its find-place. However, it was probably from the River Thames at Temple Church and was purchased from Henry Dunbar Baines. Legend has it that it came from the tomb of the Earl of Pembroke, in the Temple Church.[1]

As stated above, the blade is heavily corroded along its whole length and indeed there are three holes in places. It has been broken some 28 cm from the cross and very poorly repaired.[2] It is still possible to discern that the blade was broad, with wide fullers and stout cutting edges. The tip is almost intact. The blade construction, according to Lang and Ager, is pattern-welded and of three bands, with alternating straight and twisted sections along the length and across the width.

The hilt is typical of a Petersen type S. All faces of the crossguard retain substantial traces of silver and copper alloy decoration in the Mammen style. Patterns of interlace have been picked out in copper alloy and the interior then filled in with silver alone or a mixture of copper alloy and silver. The upper side of the crossguard, next to the grip, also has some decoration, but of a style differing from the lateral faces. The almost parallel tang is completely bound with fine silver wire, but although there are other good examples from Scandinavia, I have grave doubts whether this is the intended original covering. At each extremity of the grip is a circle of plaited silver wire which may well have helped to hold a leather grip in place. The upper guard is of a similar shape to the crossguard, but smaller. It retains some ten percent of its original decoration and most of that remaining is silver, with tiny touches of copper alloy. The five lobed pommel is separated from the lower by two strands of stout silver wire, twisted together and forced into the groove.[3] Each lobe is separated from the next by plaited silver wire bounded on each side by a string of copper alloy decorations. Sufficient decoration survives to deduce that all other areas of the pommel were originally covered with similar decoration to that on the crossguard.

[1] One worry is that the condition of the blade is not consistent with the condition of other swords, spears, spurs and metallic artifacts which have been immersed in the Thames. Indeed, the condition of the blade is more consistent with a grave find.
[2] Leslie Webster is of the opinion that the blade was damaged before deposition. *From Viking to Crusader: The Scandinavians and Europe 800 to 1200* (22nd Council of Europe Exhibition) (Copenhagen, 1992), cat. no. 413, p. 335.
[3] See especially Jan Petersen, *De Norske Vikingesverd* (Oslo, 1919) where a type S can have three or five lobes.

→ Hilt of 1887, 2-9 1 with remaining silver and copper alloy applied decoration. Photograph courtesy of and copyright British Museum.

← Full length view of 1887, 2-9 1. Photograph courtesy of and copyright British Museum.

C16430

Date: second half of the tenth century
Find-place: lake near Søborg Castle, Denmark
Overall length: 87.7 cm   *Blade length:* 73 cm
Length of cross: 10.2 cm   *Length of grip:* 9.1 cm
Balance point: 15.3 cm
Condition: generally good

It was a great joy to be in the presence of and indeed to handle this elegantly proportioned weapon, which found its way into the museum after being 'accepted by the Medieval Department as a present from Baroness Clara von Blixen-Finecke'.[1] It had been found when the lake near to Søborg Castle was drained.

This blade has a broad, 2.3 cm wide, shallow and well defined fuller on both sides which in areas is in almost pristine condition. Prominent cutting edges show some signs of honing and usage. Two areas on one side of the blade still have large fragments of the scabbard adhering to them and there is a suggestion of an iron-inlaid inscription,[2] although the main fabric of the blade is not pattern-welded.

Although at first glance, the pommel appears to be trilobated, further examination shows two additional tiny vestigial lobes for a total of five. The slim, boat-shaped crossguard bears silver inlay decoration on both lateral faces.[3] It appears to be some attempt at simple interlace, and may be related to the Mammen style.[4] The upper and lower faces of the crossguard appear to be undecorated. Similar silver decoration is present on both lateral faces of the upper guard and traces are discerned upon both sides of the three central lobes of the pommel. The larger lobe is separated from those adjacent to it by two sets of twisted silver wires. Both the beautifully tooled hilt with its delicately applied decoration and the handsome sturdy blade exist harmoniously.

Jan Petersen knew of some 25 examples of type S from Norway to which, of course, we may add the Chertsey sword and the example presently under consideration. He also knew of three examples with Ulfberht inscription to which again we may add the Chertsey sword.[5] Another type S was found in the rich tenth century grave at Gjermunbu, Norderhov, Buskerud, Norway along with a helmet, a mail shirt, riding gear and cooking equipment. The hilt of the sword was inlaid with silver and copper.[6]

[1] It was published in 1882 in Vilhelm Boye, *Fund af Gjenstande fra Old tiden og Middelalderen i og ved Søborg Sø* (Copenhagen, 1882), p. 17.
[2] This blade is an excellent candidate for an x-ray examination which will almost certainly reveal an iron-inlaid inscription or some form of decoration.
[3] The silver wire employed is approximately 0.1 cm across, allowing very fine work to be executed.
[4] Thanks are due to Anne Pedersen at the National Museum of Denmark who made this identification and drew my attention to Vilhelm Boye's book. She is also of the opinion that the decoration on these swords falls into two main groups, one which has a definite animal ornament in the Jelling style and one which has an interlace ornament which seems to be more closely related to the Mammen style. Jan Petersen does not name the style.
[5] See the great type S with an Ulfberht inscription from the National Museum of Denmark, Copenhagen, accession 780-4, pp. 100–101 herein.
[6] Universitetets Oldsaksamling, Oslo, accession C27317. See also *From Viking to Crusader*, pp. 254–255, cat. no. 108.

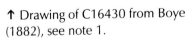

↑ Drawing of C16430 from Boye (1882), see note 1.

← Copenhagen C16430 full length view. Photograph courtesy of and copyright National Museum of Denmark.

→ Copenhagen C16430 detail of hilt showing silver wire inlay decoration. Photograph courtesy of and copyright National Museum of Denmark.

C18454, C3210 & C3211

Date: late tenth to early eleventh century
Find-place: blade, C18454, at Skoven near Mølmen at Lesjeskogen, Norway
pommel, C3210, & cross, C3211, at Korsgården Ånses., Hedemark, Norway
Overall length: 96.7 cm *Blade length:* 77.7 cm
Length of cross: 11.7 cm *Length of grip:* 9.5 cm
Condition: blade and hilt both in fine condition

So much vagueness surrounds the find-places of the component parts of this fine weapon. The museum register records the following: 'The blade of a double-edged sword of iron from the early Iron Age. Exceptionally well preserved. Length 78.5 cm. The width of the upper part 5.5 cm. The tang is naked.[1] Without the least trace of handle, and a little over 12.7 cm. long.[2] Found near Mølmen at Lesjeskogen, hidden in a cave in Skoven (18454).' A colour plate of the hilt is assigned a museum number of C18454. Yet another black and white plate showing the guard and pommel has been designated the museum numbers of C3210–11. Not even the museum staff or the museum register were able to unravel the mystery enveloping this weapon. My own feelings are that the pommel C3210 was found at Korsgården Ånses., Hedemark, probably the cross C3211 as well; both at some stage being fitted to the 'naked' blade C18454 found in a cave at Skoven.[3] Yet another entry states that 'This was the only thing found at a placed called Mølen at Lesjeskogen' (i.e. the blade).[4]

The well formed blade appears to have been regularly used in antiquity and bears several deep nicks plus much evidence of regular honing. The fullers are a little more than a third the width of the blade, and run to within 7 cm of the spatulate tip. One side of the blade is in almost mint condition and the other covered with shallow pitting, but still good. Both of the lateral faces of the boat-shaped crossguard and the trilobated pommel are almost entirely plated with silver.[5] Then 0.4 cm diameter holes 0.3 cm deep and in rows, at right angles to the blade, were drilled through the silver to expose the iron below. Each hole is surrounded by a circle, again cut through to the iron. Each little 'island' is then joined by a pair of parallel lines finely cut through the silver. Both top and bottom faces of the crossguard, the underside of the pommel and the lateral faces of the large central lobe also carry a simple interlace pattern.[5] The two tiny flanking lobes give a distinct impression of representing animal heads, possibly bears. One is badly damaged, the other almost perfect. All the extreme edges of the guards are further decorated with a cut through to the iron about 0.2 cm from the edge. This is surely one of the most striking hilts to have survived.

[1] Without a hilt.

[2] I made this measurement of 11.7 cm in July 1998.

[3] Stylistically, the crossguard and pommel are harmonious, with identical silver application and decoration. See colour plate VIII. See also Jan Petersen, *De Norske Vikingesverd* (Oslo, 1919), fig. 119.

[4] Not wishing to further confuse the situation, but, apparently when the pommel (C3210) and crossguard (C3211) were found, there were still the remains of the sword blade itself. A man made a copy of the blade, mounted it with our hilt and presented it to the University. Not our current blade, I feel.

[5] The crossguard is slightly curved towards the blade.

[6] There are also similar traces upon the crossguard faces.

← Full length view of the composite of silver covered and decorated iron hilt elements C3210 and C3211 with blade C18454. Photograph by courtesy of and copyright Universitetets Oldsaksamling, negative 5285.

National Museum of Ireland, Dublin

E122:94

Date: mid eleventh century
Find-place: Christ Church Place, Dublin, Ireland
Overall length: presently 87.4 cm *Blade length:* 75 cm
Length of cross: 9.8 cm *Length of grip:* 8.5 cm
Balance point: 19.0 cm
Condition: hilt fairly plain, in good condition, and missing the pommel; blade good with fullers and cutting edges well defined in places

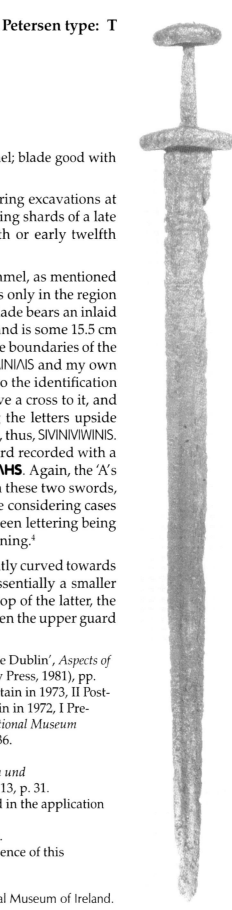

This important weapon was found in a post and wattle house during excavations at the Christ Church Place site. It was found with other items, including shards of a late Saxon tripod pitcher, which have been dated to the late eleventh or early twelfth century.[1]

The wieldability of this weapon is not good, due to loss of the pommel, as mentioned above. The well-tapered blade bears much evidence of use and it is only in the region of the tip that significant corrosion has occurred. One side of the blade bears an inlaid inscription which appears to be of silver. It begins close to the hilt and is some 15.5 cm in length. It is fairly easy to read, and is mostly contained within the boundaries of the fuller, the letters being approximately 2.0 cm high. It reads SINIMIΛINIΛIS and my own reading agrees entirely with that of Elizabeth Okasha even down to the identification of a letter where the inlay is missing.[2] As the letter 'A' does not have a cross to it, and other factors, it is possible to obtain a different reading viewing the letters upside down and starting to read from the end furthest away from the cross, thus, SIVINIVIWINIS. However, in Jorma Leppäaho's revolutionary book we have a sword recorded with a similar inscription, but in this case, iron inlaid.[3] It reads **SHVΛIMIVΛHS**. Again, the 'A's have no cross-bar. Whichever way up one reads the inscriptions on these two swords, they do not make any remnant of sense, and here again we may be considering cases whereby swords have been inscribed by swordsmiths who have seen lettering being applied but have no degree of understanding as to its overall meaning.[4]

The boat-like crossguard is of iron and appears to be hollow. It is gently curved towards the blade. The upper guard is also of iron, again is hollow and essentially a smaller version of the cross.[5] There is an incomplete plate attached to the top of the latter, the boundaries of which would have represented the decoration between the upper guard and the pommel.[6]

[1] See Elizabeth Okasha, 'Three Inscribed Objects from Christ Church Place Dublin', *Aspects of Viking Dublin, Proceedings of the Eighth Viking Congress* (Odense University Press, 1981), pp. 49–51. For further information on this sword, see J. Cherry, 'Medieval Britain in 1973, II Post-Conquest', *Med. Arch.*, XVIII (1974), p. 206. L. E. Webster, 'Medieval Britain in 1972, I Pre-Conquest', *Med. Arch.*, XVII (1973), p. 152. *Viking and Medieval Dublin: National Museum Excavation, 1962–73* (Catalogue of Exhibition) (Dublin, 1973), pp. 17 and 36.
[2] Ibid., footnote 2.
[3] Jorma Leppäaho, *Späteisenzeitliche Waffen aus Finnland: Schwertinschriften und Waffenverzierungen des 9.–12. Jahrhunderts* (Helsinki, 1964), especially tab. 13, p. 31.
[4] Or perhaps inscribed by others associated with swordsmiths and skilled in the application of inlaid inscriptions.
[5] This fairly common form of hollow hilt did little to improve the balance.
[6] It was indeed an experience of pure delight to handle and be in the presence of this important weapon.

→ Full length view of E122:94, photograph courtesy of and copyright National Museum of Ireland.

Date: tenth century
Find-place: bed of the River Lea near Edmonton, Middlesex, England
Length of cross: 12 cm *Length of grip:* 9.8 cm

It is the remains of the decoration which announces this example as being an important survivor from the tenth century. It came from the old bed of the River Lea at Edmonton, Middlesex and was donated by Sir Charles Hercules Read. Petersen knew of eight other examples found in Norway with similar hilt types, a fine example being that found at Seim Aardal.[1]

A radiographic study of the broken blade of the sword presently under consideration at the British Museum revealed double-sided iron inlaid inscriptions. The roughly symmetrical inlay on one side consists of a central plain equal-armed cross flanked on either side by an omega-like device oriented such that the looped end extends outwards from the centre of the inscription: ⌀8+8⌀. The opposite blade face inscription consists only of two transversely oriented bars. Nothing more of the pattern can be discerned.[2] Kirpichnikov shows a similar figure, but instead of a plain cross, we have a cross potent.[3] Leppäaho also illustrates two other examples, yet again, both incorporate a cross potent.[4]

The boat-shaped crossguard curves gently towards the blade and bears a chequer-board style of decoration. The whole of the surface of the crossguard's lateral faces has crosshatched scratches on the surfaces. Sufficient of the silver and copper applied metal survives to be able to ascertain precisely the form of the pattern. The grip side of the hilt was originally decorated only with copper. The proportions of this hilt are harmoniously balanced and the gently curving crossguard is complemented by a fine thin trilobated pommel made in one piece. Close examination shows that the decoration on the faces of the pommel–and some remains–was identical to that on the crossguard, and no doubt all of the separating grooves would have originally been filled with silver or copper wire, or both twisted together or even plaited.

This sword must have been strikingly beautiful in its youth and the weapon of a man of some substance. One can almost visualize the warrior proudly standing, his sword hanging in its own scabbard close to his left hip, with the rays of the sun catching the alternating facets of the copper and silver, like some jewel of war.[5]

[1] Jan Petersen, *De Norske Vikingesverd* (Oslo, 1919), pp. 153–154.
[2] Janet Lang and Barry Ager, 'Swords of the Anglo-Saxon and Viking Periods in the British Museum: a Radiographic Study', *Weapons and Warfare in Anglo-Saxon England*, ed. Sonia Chadwick Hawkes (Oxford, 1989), p. 106. These 'eyelet loops' are what I refer to as omega-like devices.
[3] A. N. Kirpichnikov, 'Drevnerusskoye oruzhiye (vyp. I) Mechi i Sabli, IX–XIII vv', *Arkheologiya SSR* (1966), pp. E1–36, specifically pl. XVIII, no. 8.
[4] Jorma Leppäaho, *Späteisenzeitliche Waffen aus Finnland: Schwertinschriften und Waffenverzierungen des 9.–12. Jahrhunderts* (Helsinki, 1964), pl. 9, no. 4 and pl. 10, no. 2.
[5] I spent a lengthy period examining this sword in November 2000. It taught me so much. For other intricately decorated hilts, refer to plates 1, 2 and 3 in the back of Petersen.

← Fig. 122 from Petersen (1919), p. 154, showing Universitetets Oldsaksamling C1779 from Seim, Aardal, N. Bergenhus, Norway.

→ Hilt of 1915.5-4.1 with remaining silver and copper alloy chequer-board style applied decoration. Photograph courtesy of and copyright British Museum.

111

Date: tenth century
Find-place: Osted, Volborg, København, Denmark
Overall length: 79.2 cm *Blade length:* 64.3 cm
Length of cross: 10.2 cm *Length of grip:* 8.8 cm
Condition: blade in a poor excavated condition; hilt remarkably well preserved.

A museum entry of 1887 indicates that this weapon was bought from a Mr. Wildmann, who found it 'on the surface of the ground'. The museum purchased it from him for 30 kroner.

The blade of this important sword was most obviously in a poor excavated condition when delivered to the museum in 1887. This poor condition and the electrolytic cleaning to which the blade was subjected has, however, miraculously unveiled the remarkable pattern-welding of the central portion of the blade and the structure of the specially hardened and fitted cutting edges.[1] The central area of the blade is constructed of two wide bands of pattern-welding in a herringbone configuration with a total combined width of 2.4 cm. This is flanked by cutting edges independently welded and with a structure flowing parallel to the blade. Analytical research has shown that on some blades of this period (and before), the smith had acquired skills whereby he could apply an even harder, tougher covering to the main body of the cutting edge.[2]

We have discussed the fine physical qualities of the blade, but it is the true beauty of the decoration upon the hilt which announces the importance of this weapon. Fortunately, the hilt was not subjected to the same form of cleaning. The pommel is trilobated and the larger central lobe is almost entirely covered in close patterns of twisted silver wire with alternate rows reversed, hammered onto the surface of the parent metal. This style of decoration is highly effective especially as the hilt is turned to a light source where all the angled facets of its herringbone decoration exude quality.[3] The flanking lobes of the pommel also bear traces of similar decoration, as indeed does the upper guard. The deep channels between the lobes are empty, but must have also at one time contained the very commonly seen twisted silver wire or some similar decoration, perhaps a beaded silver strip. There is sufficient decoration remaining on one lateral side of the crossguard to deduce that it too was also completely silver encased with identical decoration to the upper hilt. In conclusion, this is a weapon of princely status.

[1] This harsh cleaning process almost certainly destroyed other important details.
[2] Two blades of c. 700 have recently been analysed using non-destructive methods. The results showed that hardened pieces of steel had been welded onto the basic form of the cutting edge. That this could be accomplished, at this early date, with no more than a simple forge and basic tools is quite remarkable.
[3] To have these twisted strands of silver wire adhering to the base metal of the hilt elements for so many centuries must point to a very sophisticated technique of application. For similar decoration see Johs. Bøe, 'Norse Antiquities in Ireland', *Viking Antiquities in Great Britain and Ireland, Part III*, ed. Haakon Shetelig (Oslo, 1940), p. 13 and fig. 1, the sword found at Island-Bridge, Dublin, being museum number WK-15.

← C5818 full length view. Photograph courtesy of and copyright National Museum of Denmark, negative III 339.

→ C5818 detail of hilt. Photograph courtesy of and copyright National Museum of Denmark.

113

Petersen type V

This type may be characterized as having a relatively tall trilobate pommel, 3 to 4 cm in height, and straight guards. The maximum thickness of the pommel remains about the same as that of the upper guard The transitions between the lobes of the pommel are subtle, and while the outline of the pommel is not perfectly elliptical, it is quite rounded when compared with types such as R, S and T. Also typical is an applied decorative covering over the guards and pommel using silver and or bronze in a stepped pattern. Twined wires may accentuate the divisions between the upper guard and pommel and between the pommel lobes.

Petersen placed this type in the earlier part of the tenth century and suggested a relationship with the earlier types D and E. All of the associated blades in his series were double-edged. Though concentrated in the east within Norway, the type has a very broad European distribution, as may be seen plotted in Jakobsson.

Mikael Jakobsson, *Krigarideologi och vikingatida svärdstypologi* (Stockholm, 1992), pp. 213, 227.

Jan Petersen, *De Norske Vikingesverd* (Oslo, 1919), pp. 154–156.

← Pl. III, B2799, from Jan Petersen, *De Norske Vikingesverd* (Oslo, 1919), captioned Torblaa Ulvik S.B.

Petersen type W

This type is set apart from the following type X in that the hilt elements are made of bronze rather than iron. The upper hilt of this type consists only of a pommel, however, decorative grooves recall earlier types having a three lobed pommel atop an upper guard. The pommel has a semicircular profile and is relatively flat. Various repetitive motifs cover the surfaces apart from the lines and may be made up of various lines and or circular markings.

Of the few examples in Petersen's series which retained blades, all of the blades were double-edged. Most examples have been recovered from Norway, though sporadic finds have been recorded from Sweden, Russia and England. Petersen dates this type to the first half of the tenth century upon the basis of associated finds and similarities with some earlier examples of type X.

Mikael Jakobsson, *Krigarideologi och vikingatida svärdstypologi* (Stockholm, 1992), pp. 213, 228.

← Fig. 123, T3107, from Jan Petersen, *De Norske Vikingesverd* (Oslo, 1919), pp. 156–158, captioned Bredvold, Aafjorden, S.T.

Fig. 123. Bredvold, Aafjorden, S. T. ½.

C8727

Date: first half of the tenth century to the middle of the eleventh century
Find-place: Tissø, Ars, Holbæk, Denmark
Overall length: 89.2 cm   *Blade length:* 75.4 cm
Length of cross: 11.9 cm   *Length of grip:* 9 cm
Balance point: 17 cm
Condition: excellent for excavated specimen

The sword under examination, found in a lake near Tissø, was sent in to the museum by Captain G. A. Friis on behalf of 'batchelor' Khristian Larsen who received the princely sum of 50 kroner in the year of 1896. The overall proportions of this fine example are positively eye-catching and it is strikingly similar to a pattern-welded sword found with a large number of other objects at Camp de Péran, Côtes-d'Armor, France, in a 10th century context.[1] Two other excellent examples of this type may be seen exhibited at the Musée de l'Armée, Paris.[2]

The blade still retains well-defined cutting edges and fullers, the latter being extremely shallow with vague boundaries and are approximately 2.4 cm wide. The two weapons from Paris, mentioned above, are both pattern-welded and there are fairly strong signs pointing to this Tissø sword being both pattern-welded and carrying an iron inlaid inscription and designs as with Oakeshott X.4.[3]

The hilt with its small but dainty 'D' or 'tea-cosy' shaped pommel and simple rather thin cross is of plain iron. Halos of corrosion products accurately pinpoint the extent of the old grip.[4]

To date, this excellent weapon has received no form of conservation, but there is no doubt that upon completion of that process, the Nationalmuseet will be in possession of a sword of some distinction. Petersen states that there are two variants of this type and this sword from Tissø is of the uncommon and earlier type.[5]

[1] See *From Viking to Crusader: The Scandinavians and Europe 800 to 1200* (22nd Council of Europe Exhibition) (Copenhagen, 1992), p. 321, cat. no. 359. Other finds included two spearheads, one of which may well be pattern-welded, an axe, an iron pot and a silver coin identified as a St. Peter penny of York Vikings, dated c. 905–925.
[2] Museum numbers JPO 2253 and JPO 2251, included herein on pp. 118–119 and 120–121, respectively, which most closely resembles the Copenhagen example. See also museum number 1372 in Nationalmuseet, Copenhagen.
[3] Ewart Oakeshott, *Records of the Medieval Sword* (Woodbridge, 1991), p. 24.
[4] See Jan Petersen, *De Norske Vikingesverd* (Oslo, 1919), pp. 158–167 for other examples of type X swords.
[5] For more details on type X see NM 2033:1 the sword from Padasjoki, Finland, on pp. 122–123 herein.

→ Copenhagen C8727 full length view. Photograph courtesy of and copyright National Museum of Denmark, negative III 339.

C26494

Date: tenth century
Find-place: Skatteby farm, Rogne parish, Østre Slidre, Valdres, Oppland, Norway
Overall length: 94.8 cm   *Blade length:* 79.8 cm
Length of cross: 16.3 cm   *Length of grip:* 9.0 cm
Balance point: 13.8 cm
Condition: hilt excellent with light pitting, blade generally well preserved, but slightly bent and with one small hole close to the tip

This remarkable sword was found in a tenth century male grave on Skatteby farm, Rogne parish, Østre Slidre, Valdres, Oppland county. According to the museum register, it was found in 1936 while digging the foundations of a house. A small mound of stone, half a metre high was discovered at the bottom of another mound, next to a big stone. The grave also yielded a fine shield boss and a spearhead, both of which had been damaged prior to burial. The spearhead has *glødeskall*. The finely tapered blade, 5.8 cm wide at the cross, is mostly in excellent condition, with well-defined shallow fullers and wide cutting edges, the former occupying slightly less than one third of the entire width and running to a point some 19 cm from the tip where some corrosion has occurred, causing a central longitudinal hole and a small crack.[1]

The massive hilt is strikingly beautiful, especially as it is so simply decorated, with all lateral faces of the pommel and crossguard covered with lines of tiny drilled holes, an average 0.2 cm in diameter and 0.6 cm apart.[2] The long boat-shaped crossguard curves gently towards the handsome blade and the extremities of both lateral faces are marked with a narrow groove, acting as a pair of borders to the arrays of lined-up holes. The solid tea-cosy type pommel is divided into two sections by a groove, the bottom being the larger, and the top curved portion is further divided into three lobes, again by single grooves cut into the iron. There is also a single decorative cut at the boundary of the lower half of the pommel.

Up until the publication of his book, Petersen reported that 49 of type X had been found, with a fairly even distribution across the whole country. Of that number, only two had single-edged blades.[3] Jakobsson reports 198 examples of type X and illustrates a broad distribution over northwestern Europe.[4]

The gentle curve at the base of the pommel, the graceful curve of the massively long crossguard towards the elegant blade, the robust stout tang, the harmony of all the elements of the hilt with the blade, the fine balance and feel of the weapon, when handled; all of these qualities and more make this sword one of the very finest to have endured the rigours of time.[5]

[1] Though the blade is slightly bent at the point of the crack, I do not think the sword had been 'ritually killed', as indeed the spear and shield boss appear to have been.
[2] For a similar hilt type see Jan Petersen, *De Norske Vikingesverd* (Oslo, 1919), p. 159, fig. 125.
[3] See Petersen, p. 162.
[4] Mikael Jakobsson, *Krigarideologi och vikingatida svärdstypologi* (Stockholm, 1992), pp. 213–214 and 228.
[5] Lee Jones and I inspected this exceptional weapon together in 1993 and in 1998 I had the joy of handling it again.

↑ Detail of the hilt of C26494 showing the shallow inscribed lines upon a pommel made as a single piece, recalling earlier forms with a separate upper guard and lobulated pommel. Photograph courtesy of and copyright Universitetets Oldsaksamling, negative 15693.

← Full length view of C26494. Photograph by Eirik Irgens Johnsen courtesy of and copyright Universitetets Oldsaksamling, negative 23350A.

JPO 2253

Date: tenth century
Overall length: 94.2 cm *Blade length:* 79.1 cm
Length of cross: 10.3 cm *Length of grip:* 10.2 cm
Balance point: 15.0 cm
Condition: excavated condition, well conserved

This must have been a stunning weapon to behold, in its youth. Even now its long grip and well-proportioned cross and pommel complement the long slender blade, in such a manner to announce the presence of a very special weapon.[1]

The blade has two central bands of pattern-welding, flanked by the cutting edges. For this type to be pattern-welded in the context of the Norwegian material is extremely rare, for of the 49 swords of this type known to Petersen, none were pattern-welded.

The corrosion has occurred uniformly and thus allows us to see, with some clarity, the structure of blade, its central section and both cutting edges. It does appear that we have an excellent example of the *blodiða* style of pattern-welding through the central portion of the blade.[2] The blade had been broken and re-welded in antiquity, at a distance of some 30 cm from the tip.

The cross is robust, square in cross-section with simple rounded ends and is pieced by a sturdy tang, to which is attached a large and weighty D shaped pommel measuring 7 cm in width and 3.8 cm in height.

The latter is circumscribed by a saw cut into which a silver latten or iron wire would have been forced as a simple form of decoration.[3]

When considering this weapon, it would be wise to consider the footnotes to sword JPO 2251 on pp. 120–121 from the same collection and also to read the description of sword NM 2033:1 from Padasjoki, Finland on pp. 122–123, for more details on type X.

[1] There is an almost identically hilted sword in the Musée de Cluny, museum no. CL 8607. It has a marginally smaller pommel and slightly longer cross.
[2] For a fine example of this, see the beautifully pattern-welded sword on pp. 26–27. See also R. Ewart Oakeshott, *The Archaeology of Weapons* (London, 1960), fig. 70.
[3] Sometimes a single strand would be used or two strands twisted together, or alternately a beaded strip.

← Full length view of JPO 2253 showing a gently tapering blade. Photograph courtesy of and copyright Musée de l'Armée, Paris, negative K23720.

→ Hilt of JPO 2253 showing a 'tea-cosy' pommel with a circumferential groove giving the appearance of an upper guard matching the height of the crossguard. Photograph courtesy of and copyright Musée de l'Armée, Paris, negative K23721.

119

JPO 2251

Date: mid tenth through mid eleventh century
Overall length: 87.8 cm *Blade length:* 73.8 cm
Length of cross: 10.4 cm *Length of grip:* 9.4 cm
Balance point: 14.9 cm
Condition: excavated with focally severe corrosion

This is another nicely tapering slender-bladed, exquisitely proportioned weapon dominated by a massively wide tang and dating from c. 950 to 1050.

The blade of this well-balanced weapon is in a fine state of preservation with some areas well nurtured by time. This was a well-used blade with deep nicks along both cutting edges.[1]

Both the cutting edges and the fullers retain good form and there exists the remnants of an iron-inlaid inscription or pattern on both sides of the blade.

It is certain that some inlay has been lost and almost all is indecipherable apart from two bars at right-angles to the length of the blade, like **II** followed by a pattern of interlace. This is very reminiscent of Ulfberht's pattern, which accompanies his name, but with so little evidence remaining, it is so easy to give a wrong reading. The extreme tip of the blade is bent back upon itself as shown in the illustration of the whole sword.

As already mentioned, the tiny 'D' shaped pommel (5.7 cm in length and 2.5 cm thick) has one face almost totally uncorroded.[2]

The cross is of a simple square cross-section with rounded ends.

This exciting weapon is almost identical to the sword illustrated on plate 2 in Leppäaho[3] which has a similar pattern to that associated with Ulfberht upon one side of the blade and the inscription **DUNA + DUNA XX** upon the other; all of the lettering and design picked out in pattern-welding.

This yet again is one of the great treasures of the Musée de l'Armée.

---

[1] Some of these 'nicks' have been accentuated by corrosion, which is a common phenomenon.
[2] This is a Petersen type X. See Jan Petersen, *De Norske Vikingesverd* (Oslo, 1919), pp. 158–161. Also, for an almost identical type, refer to C8727 in the Nationalmuseet, Copenhagen reserve collection, described herein on pp. 115–116.
[3] See Jorma Leppäaho, *Späteisenzeitliche Waffen aus Finnland: Schwertinschriften und Waffenverzierungen des 9.–12. Jahrhunderts* (Helsinki, 1964), p. 8 and pl. 2, sword NM8120 and for a model with a smaller pommel, sword NM11840, p. 14, and pl. 5, examples 2a, b, c, d, and e.

← Full length view of JPO 2251 showing a gently tapering blade with a spatulate tip. Photograph courtesy of and copyright Musée de l'Armée, Paris, negative K23706.

→ Hilt of JPO 2251 showing the 'tea-cosy' pommel. Photograph courtesy of and copyright Musée de l'Armée, Paris, negative K23707.

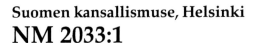

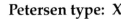

NM 2033:1

Date: second half of the tenth century
Find-place: Padasjoki, Finland
Overall length: 90.1 cm   *Blade length:* 77.6 cm
Length of cross: 18.6 cm   *Length of grip:* 8.9 cm
Balance point: 20.1 cm
Condition: a certain amount of shallow overall pitting on the hilt and a similar degree of corrosion on the blade, but with one area in almost pristine condition

This elegant weapon has one of those finely tapering and beautifully proportioned blades, thin in section and yet, in conjunction with a somewhat tiny pommel, capable of producing an excellent degree of balance. The blade, which has undulations along its whole length probably due to differing degrees of corrosion, carries a central fuller on each side tapering from approximately 2.1 cm to 1 cm in width and terminating about 9 cm from the point. One central portion of the blade is in almost pristine condition. Yet again, the tang is of a remarkably robust character, thus imparting great strength to the hilt. On one side of the blade is a very fine inscription inlaid in iron and filling the full width of the fuller, at that point approximately 1.9 cm in width. The inscription reads **INLERURIEITI** and may well have had some important meaning or significance in antiquity. It may well be that a skilled, but illiterate swordsmith had seen other blades bearing inscriptions and had sought to bedeck his own in a similar fashion, stringing a series of letters together in an incomprehensible manner. Conversely, each letter could be the first in a sequence of words forming some kind of religious invocation. On the other side of the blade, despite more heavy corrosion, it is just possible to detect another iron inlaid inscription or series of devices, but not possible to identify the lettering apart from a letter **M** and the remains of an omega.[1] The fullers and cutting edges remain well defined, the former being fully capable even now of taking an edge. The delicately tapered cross is gently curved towards the blade and of a type which the Vikings called *gaddhjalt* or spikehilt. The tiny 'tea-cosy' in transition to 'brazil nut' pommel remains in fine condition and successfully completes the appearance of this handsome hilt. The whole appearance of this weapon is reminiscent of the hauntingly beautiful Ingelrii sword in the Glasgow museum.[2]

According to Petersen this type spans an extensive time period, namely from the first half of the 10th century to the middle of the 11th century. He further states that it appears in two variants. The older has a taller and slimmer pommel, while the cross is thicker (in profile) and slightly curved. The later and more common of the two variants has a lower thicker and shorter pommel and a less thick, but longer cross, which can be up to 18 cm in length.[3] Petersen knew of 49 specimens of this type and quite evenly distributed across the whole of Norway. The earlier group comprised only 9 specimens whereas the later group totalled 40. Forty-five are double-edged, 2 single-edged and 2 cannot be determined. Apparently, on a couple of blades there are inlaid marks (not letters) but none were pattern-welded.[4]

[1] See Jorma Leppäaho, *Späteisenzeitliche Waffen aus Finnland: Schwertinschriften und Waffenverzierungen des 9.–12. Jahrhunderts* (Helsinki, 1964), p. 14 and pl. 5, 1a–c.

[2] See specifically Ewart Oakeshott, *Sword in the Age of Chivalry* (London, 1964), pl. IC. and Ian Peirce, 'The Development of the Medieval Sword, c. 850–1300', *Ideals and Practice of Medieval Knighthood: Papers from the Third Strawberry Hill Conference*, ed. C. Harper-Bill and Ruth Harvey (Woodbridge, 1988), pp. 145–146 and pl. 5. It must be remembered that it was Ewart Oakeshott, who once owned this splendid sword, who first revealed and identified the Ingelrii inscription; a description of the unorthodox means by which this inscription was revealed appears in Ewart Oakeshott, *Records of the Medieval Sword* (Woodbridge, 1991), p. 27.

[3] See Jan Petersen, *De Norske Vikingesverd* (Oslo, 1919), fig. 125, which is the earlier type, and compare with the example under consideration.

[4] See Jaap Ypey, 'Einige wikingerzeitliche Schwerter aus den Niederlanden', *Offa* 41 (1984), p. 224 and fig. 7 and Oakeshott *Records* (1991), p. 24, sword X.4. There are an increasing number of Viking age swords being described which are pattern-welded and also have iron inlaid inscriptions, patterns or devices.

← Helsinki 2033:1 full length view. Photograph by E. Laakso (1947) courtesy of and copyright National Museum of Finland, negative 14329.

→ Helsinki 2033:1 detail of hilt. Photograph by E. Laakso (1947) courtesy of and copyright National Museum of Finland, negative 14812, previously published in Leppäaho, p. 15, pl. 5, 1a.

↓ Helsinki 2033:1 photograph of blade inscription. Photograph courtesy of and copyright National Museum of Finland, negative 28002, previously published in Leppäaho, p. 15, pl. 5, 1c.; the inscription on the reverse side is also illustrated as pl. 5, 1b.

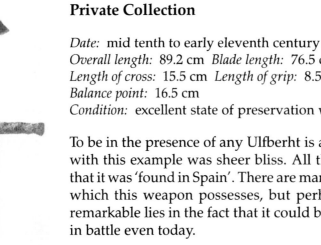

Date: mid tenth to early eleventh century
Overall length: 89.2 cm *Blade length:* 76.5 cm
Length of cross: 15.5 cm *Length of grip:* 8.5 cm
Balance point: 16.5 cm
Condition: excellent state of preservation with all inlay intact

To be in the presence of any Ulfberht is a moment to cherish, but to meet up with this example was sheer bliss. All that we know of its recent history is that it was 'found in Spain'. There are many outstanding features and qualities which this weapon possesses, but perhaps the most important and most remarkable lies in the fact that it could be drawn from its scabbard and used in battle even today.

It is a beautifully balanced sword and possesses those elegant proportions which prevail when the blade is almost parallel for some seventy percent of its length before tapering begins. The fullers are equally well preserved, retaining much of their original form and occupy about half of the blade width. This blade had been well used during its 'life', which probably began c. 950.[1] The cutting edges show much evidence of honing and bear numerous battle scars.[2] Again, most amazingly, the point is completely intact, as befits such a unique weapon.[3] The blade is as straight as a die.

On one side of the blade is a handsomely executed **+ULFBERHT+** inscription, with all of the pattern-welded inlay intact and as firmly embedded and sound as the day it was set in place. Upon the reverse side is dear old Ulfberht's characteristic lattice pattern between parallel lines and again with all inlay complete.[4]

Ulfberht, whoever he was, or those very sophisticated craftsmen who followed in his footsteps, probably his sons and grandsons and great grandsons (or daughters and granddaughters and greatgranddaughters) and so on, had realized the importance of backing-up the blade signature with a logo.

A final word upon this weapon. The massively long cross, the hugely wide pommel and sturdy tang somehow complete the poetic equation which announces this example to be a very special weapon. All the proportions are right to the eye, especially the fact that the pommel width is more than the blade width and one can only be in awe of the weaponsmith who realized the effect upon the eye of causing the cross to curve gently towards the blade.

[1] Evidence of sculpture shows that this pommel type was used well into the twelfth century, even up to c. 1200. See the illustrations of the font from Verona.
[2] This blade would have been much wider in its youth as indicated by the tell-tale signs of honing, regular sharpening from the crossguard to the end of the Ulfberht inscription. The total length of Ulfberht inscription is 18.5 cm.
[3] A great rarity, as due to the thinness of the metal at the tip it is more quickly eroded away.
[4] See Jorma Leppäaho, *Späteisenzeitliche Waffen aus Finnland: Schwertinschriften und Waffenverzierungen des 9.–12. Jahrhunderts* (Helsinki, 1964), pp. 36–37 for an Ulfberht pattern-welded inscription very similar to that under examination.

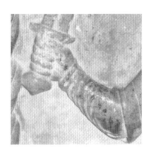

← Overall view of the side of the sword bearing an Ulfberht inscription. Photograph by Sylvia Oliver.

→ Hilt from the side of the sword opposite the Ulfberht inscription showing the brazil nut pommel and gently down-curved crossguard. Photograph by Sylvia Oliver.

↙ Detail from a massive carved marble font, c. 1200, in an ancient baptistry at Verona, Italy. Photograph by Ian Peirce.

↓ Details of the pattern-welded iron inlaid Ulfberht inscription and the geometric latticework design on the opposite face of the blade. Photographs by Sylvia Oliver.

C18798

Date: tenth century
Find-place: Rygnestad farm, Valle Sogn, Nedenes, Norway
Overall length: 93.2 cm *Blade length:* 78.2 cm
Length of cross: 13.8 cm *Length of grip:* 10.3 cm
Condition: badly corroded in places, but some areas are in pristine condition

This unusual tenth century weapon was found on a farm called Rygnestad in Valle Sogn and the register has these details under an entry for 1897.

It is a great rarity to see a tenth century sword with such an acutely tapered blade, and this example is not unlike the great sword from the River Great Ouse, Stretham, near to Ely.[1] Although it is corroded through in places, the last 44 cm of the sword presently under consideration are in a fairly healthy state, and in places, the fullers and cutting edges are in a fine state of preservation.

The hilt is rather imposing with its massive and sturdy Indian canoe-like crossguard. The huge tapered tang is terminated with a cocked-hat style pommel equally as sturdy as the crossguard. Some attempt has been made at applying decoration for just below the upper edge of the lateral faces of the pommel, a 0.6 cm wide channel has been gouged. This feature is more easily seen on Petersen's fig. 130. Often for these swords of type Y, the upper hilt is made in two pieces[2] and again very often the upper element, or pommel, has been lost leaving quite simply a curved bar, as in the case of the fine single-edged sword from Godbrandsdal, Oppland.

All but one of the 18 swords with this hilt type listed by Jan Petersen have double-edged blades. Having an unusually finely tapered blade, this sword likely would have possessed excellent wieldability.

[1] See R. Ewart Oakeshott, *Records of the Medieval Sword* (Woodbridge, 1991), p. 74.
[2] Jan Petersen, *De Norske Vikingesverd* (Oslo, 1919), figs. 131–132.

↓ Full length view of C18798. Photograph by Leif Pedersen courtesy of and copyright Universitetets Oldsaksamling, negative 21583/18.

NM2886:11

Date: middle of the eleventh century
Find-place: Vesilahti, Sakoinen, Hukari, Finland
Overall length: 87.2 cm *Blade length:* 72 cm (incomplete)
Length of cross: 12.4 cm *Length of grip:* 7.4 cm
Condition: blade is broken 32.5 cm from the hilt and much of both sides of the blade are in almost mint condition and exhibit the precisely defined boundaries of the fullers and cutting edges

The broken off lower portion of this blade is badly corroded, but sufficient of it remains to establish, beyond any doubt, its shape and character. Here we have an acutely pointed blade, which must have given this weapon an unusually fine balance in the hand of its owner. The fullers are deeply cut into the blade to a depth of some 0.15 cm and, together with the cutting edges, are in almost mint condition to a point of some 9 cm from the hilt on one side and all of the first 28 cm on the reverse side.[1] There are no signs of any iron inlay or any form of decoration on the blade.

Leppäaho remarked that the hilt was originally silver-plated but had been 'greatly spoiled by fire'.[2] A translation of Leppäaho's text regarding the method of application of the silver ornamentation is not entirely clear, but it would appear that the parent metal of the hilt had received its design by the careful use of a fine chisel, accompanied by numerous scratches on the surface, onto which the applied sheets of silver could be hammered and consequently be attached. This unusual style of cross does in fact still retain ornamentation on four sites: the central field and right hand arm on one lateral face and the central field and left hand arm on the other.[3] The former side's central field has a 'Maltese style' cross chiselled neatly into the surface and is almost identical to the cross in the same position on the reverse side. The decoration on the other two sites, which may have had some significance in Viking times, defies description and in reality is not quite as simple as illustrated in Leppäaho. There is also a smaller Maltese cross incised with great precision into the central field of the lower element of the pommel and this area appears to have retained some silver plating. Indeed, the five lobes of the pommel do still exhibit areas of silver, but the decoration is badly worn, possibly a consequence of fire damage. The pommel is most beautifully crafted and is similar to two other swords of Petersen type Z from Loken, Hole, Busk and Hafstem, Gransherred, BRB., and another, made of bronze in the British Museum.[4]

[1] It is indeed most rare to inspect a weapon (as Lee Jones and I did in 1994) which still retains its original surface. Other good examples are, of course, the sword of Sancho the IV of Castille and the splendid A459 in the Wallace collection.
[2] Jorma Leppäaho, *Späteisenzeitliche Waffen aus Finnland: Schwertinschriften und Waffenverzierungen des 9.–12. Jahrhunderts* (Helsinki, 1964), p. 78, pl. 37. Leppäaho's mention of fire and the fact that areas of the hilt and blade are in pristine condition must mean that *glødeskall* is exhibited.
[3] Leppäaho comments that the ornamentation was made more visible by the application of aluminium oxide. See Leppäaho, pl. 37.
[4] Jan Petersen, *De Norske Vikingesverd* (Oslo, 1919) , pp. 175–177. Note that both of these weapons illustrated in Petersen have extremely slim tangs, like 2886:11.

↗ Helsinki 2886:11 full view. Photograph by E. Laakso (1955) courtesy of and copyright National Museum of Finland, negative 18671.

JPO 2242

Date: first half of the eleventh century, silver inlay probably later
Overall length: 100.4 cm *Blade length:* 86 cm
Length of cross: 17.3 cm *Length of grip:* 9.1 cm
Balance point: 21 cm
Condition: both blade and hilt in an excellent state of preservation

It was a source of great joy for me to handle, examine and record the many attributes of this remarkable weapon, both in 1993 and again in 1995.[1] Prior to 1993 it had not been examined closely or rigorously. Even without its totally intact, intricate, puzzling and beautifully executed silver inlays, this sword would feature among the top ten survivors of its period. This beautifully decorated sword is in such a robust physical condition that, should the need arise, it could be used today.[2]

The very long, slender blade swiftly tapers from a point some 43 cm from the hilt and has shallow fullers running to within 15 cm of the point. The cross is long and thin with a slight taper. The broad acutely tapered tang terminates with a well-preserved type B pommel which is almost 2 inches (4.9 cm) across. It appears that all of the silver inlay upon the blade remains intact. An interpretation of the meaning of all the strange figures and devices upon both

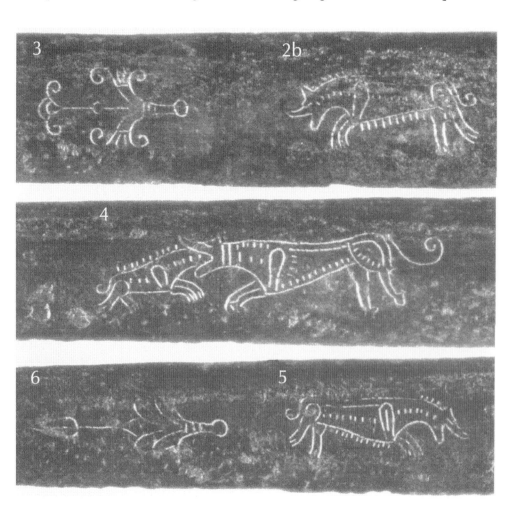

faces of this blade, and indeed the blades of the others mentioned below, may be difficult, especially if they are actually a randomly collected series of decorations being 'the work of an individual or a group of craftsmen, with ideas of their own, doodling on the blades they are given to decorate'.[3] Putting this explanation aside, however, it may be possible to explain one or two elements.

One side of the blade has more decoration than the other. Starting at the cross we have:

1. A roundel with an eagle-like bird perched within it.

2. A large wolf-like creature devouring a snake; the personification of evil is often expressed by the presence of a snake.

3. A roundel, the same size as the first above, inside of which is a perched bird.

4. A small off-centre letter N.

5. An unusual winged creature with a tiny head and a fish-like tail.

6. A smaller letter N as above.

7. A roundel with a bird-like creature inside followed by two tiny circles.

8. A parmette design almost identical to that on the River Bann blade.

9. A roundel in which is a marigold-like flower; often used as a symbol of Christ.

10. A small dove-like bird in flight.

11. This shape, ⊏ , at right angles to the length of the blade.

12. A reversed letter 'S' inside a small circle, ⊚ .

Upon the reverse side and illustrated on the opposite page:

1. A parmette design.

2. A large wolf-like creature (2b) which is being chased by a small wolf-like animal.

3. A symmetrical design very similar to that upon the blades of many mid eighteenth century small swords.

4. A large wolf-like creature devouring a small dog-like animal.

5. A large wolf-like creature chasing a small dog-like creature, the latter being almost identical to that in #4, and

6. A smaller version of the design in #3 above.

Almost all of the wolf-like creatures closely resemble those to be found in the lower border of that unique pictorial source, the Bayeux tapestry.[4] Yet again with diligence, and again in the lower border, we may find an unusual winged creature with a tiny head and fish-like tail so similar to that image found upon the blade.[5] There are at least eight other weapons, both complete and fragmentary, which have similar fine inlay decoration, either in silver, latten, gold or copper. Two were found in Switzerland, one at Yverdon and the other in the lake at Neuenburg.[6] Another is from Leikkimäki, Kokemäki, Finland where all of the extensive inlay is in gold.[7] Much work needs to be done to better understand the decoration upon the blades of this important group of swords.

This Finnish weapon is one of 17 whole or incomplete swords with similar hilt types, many found with silver decorated spearheads. Two were found in Ireland, one from the River Bann and a splendid example from the River Blackwater. Another three incomplete specimens are from Holland, one from the Waal near Nyjmegen, one from the lower Rhine at Rees and one from Lummada on the island of Osel.[8] This remarkable sword, from Paris, as a whole, probably dates from circa 1000 to 1050 but I have a strong feeling that the silver inlay was applied later, perhaps in the late eleventh to early twelfth century.

← Overall view of JPO 2242 in Paris. Photograph courtesy of and copyright Musée de l'Armée, Paris; negative K 23722.

← Details from the blade of JPO 2242, enlarged from the adjacent photograph and with enhanced contrast.

↑ Detail of the hilt of Paris JPO 2242. Photograph courtesy of and copyright Musée de l'Armée, Paris; negative K 23723.

[1] Thanks are due to Jean-Paul Sage-Frenay of the Departement des Armes et Armures, Musée de l'Armée, Paris for *many kindnesses and help.*

[2] This sword is to be subject of an in-depth study by the author, sometime in the near future.

[3] See Ewart Oakeshott, *Records of the Medieval Sword* (Woodbridge, 1991), p. 47.

[4] See Sir Frank Stenton, et al., *The Bayeux Tapestry* (1957), pl. 4.

[5] Ibid, pls. 20 and 23.

[6] Collection, Schweizerisiches Landesmuseum, museum no. LM 10116 and IN 7002. See also Hugo Schneider, *Waffen im Schweizerischen Landesmuseum: Griffwaffen I* (Zürich, 1980), p. 22, #16 and p. 23, #17, respectively, where these swords are illustrated and dated to 1150 to 1250.

[7] Collection, Helsinki University, museum no. NM 1174:1 (see p. 138 herein).

[8] Collection, National Museum of Ireland, Dublin, museum no. WK.48. Found buried in the sand in the bar or shoal between Tome and Greagh, the ancient ford of the River Bann between the counties of Derry and Antrim. See Johs. Bøe, 'Norse Antiquities in Ireland', *Viking Antiquities in Great Britain and Ireland, Part III,* ed. Haakon Shetelig (Oslo, 1940), pp. 83–84, pl. 56. The other sword was recovered during dredging operations in the River Blackwater, between the townlands of Copney, Co. Armagh and Derrygally, Co. Tyrone. It was found in 1974 and taken to the Ulster Museum. Because there are several rivers named Blackwater in Ireland it was decided it would be called the 'Copney-Derrygally Sword'. See also Oakeshott, *Records*, pp. 45–51.

Musée de l'Armée, Paris
JPO 2241

Oakeshott type: Xa

Date: mid tenth century to mid eleventh century
Overall length: 102.7 cm *Blade length:* 88.7 cm
Length of cross: 19.8 cm *Length of grip:* 9.7 cm
Balance point: 22.1 cm
Condition: A river find without any doubt, with some areas of the blade cross and delightfully sculptured pommel showing original surfaces.

Just a brief glimpse of this weapon and one is reminded of the great Ingelrii, now in the Glasgow Collection but once in the care of Ewart Oakeshott, who discovered its inscription.[1]

This elegant, finely tapering blade has well-formed fullers running down to within a few centimetres of the point. The cutting edges are also in good condition and bear much evidence of use. On one side of the blade, set within the fuller (at a distance of approximately 10.0 cm from the cross) is a cross-potent: ✠. This may well precede an inscription and on the same side of the blade, just halfway down, there appears to be an 'O' or an omega, but the inlay is missing. There also appears to be evidence of an iron-inlaid inscription upon the reverse side.[2]

The length of the blade is longer than the average and is, for example, some 11.0 cm longer than the Glasgow sword.

The long (almost 20.0 cm or 8 inches) narrow and gently tapering cross is of a type known by the Vikings as *gaddhjalt* or spike-hilt and the added length would have given the hand of the warrior considerably more protection without overly increasing the weight.

The tang is stout, with a minute taper and terminates with a beautifully preserved walnut style pommel, which boasts its original surface.

This weapon conveys a most-powerful presence and should be compared with the splendid example (which is even larger) published by Jorma Leppäaho and which also appears within this volume.[3]

It is also true to state that all weapons with this style of hilt seem to demand one's attention.

[1] Ewart Oakeshott, *Records of the Medieval Sword* (Woodbridge, 1991), pp. 27 and 32. See also Ian Peirce, 'The Development of the Medieval Sword, c. 850–1300', *Ideals and Practice of Medieval Knighthood: Papers from the Third Strawberry Hill Conference (1988)*, ed. C. Harper-Bill and Ruth Harvey, pp. 139–158 and in particular 145 to 146 and pl. 5. Also Ewart Oakeshott, *The Sword in the Age of Chivalry, Revised Edition* (London, 1981), p. 29 and pl. 1c.
[2] Crosses often precede and end an inscription.
[3] Namely NM 2033:1 in Jorma Leppäaho, *Späteisenzeitliche Waffen aus Finnland: Schwertinschriften und Waffenverzierungen des 9.–12. Jahrhunderts* (Helsinki, 1964), p. 14 and pl. 5.

→ Full view of JPO 2241. Photograph courtesy of and copyright Musée de l'Armée, Paris; negative K 23724.

Suomen kansallismuse, Helsinki
Oakeshott type: Xa
NM 11840

Date: late tenth century to middle of the eleventh century
Find-place: Vammala (formerly Tryvää) railway station, Finland
Overall length: 98.3 cm *Blade length:* 84.9 cm
Length of cross: 13.8 cm *Length of grip:* 9.7 cm
Balance point: 18.3 cm
Condition: some deep surface pitting upon the blade and crossguard; the pommel is in an excellent state of preservation with some small areas of light pitting

This is a most elegant weapon, much due to the acutely tapered line of the blade. A narrow fuller, some 0.2 cm deep at the proximal end, runs to within some 14 cm of the point on both sides of the blade. It carries a misspelt Innominidomini iron inlaid inscription on one side of the blade, characteristically set between two crosses potent, within a narrow fuller which is 1.3 to 1.1 cm in width. It is clearly visible and almost all of the iron inlay remains. The actual inscription reads **+INNOMNEDHI+** and mirrors that seen and recorded by Jorma Leppäaho. On the reverse side is another inscription, which after a lengthy examination in June 1994, Dr. Lee Jones concluded to be **+NSOMEFECIT+** and *not* as recorded in Leppäaho.[1] There are at least three other swords inscribed with **+NISOMEFECIT+**; another in Helsinki, one in private hands, and the last in the museum at Stade.[2] According to Leppäaho, the inscriptions on the sword under consideration are damascened. The cutting edges remain well defined especially towards the proximal end of the blade.

The crossguard is simply a gently tapering bar of iron, crudely pierced to take the long, robust tang. The pommel is tiny and yet most precisely formed, being of a 'tea-cosy' type in transition to a 'brazil nut'. Overall, the hilt is plain, carrying no form of decoration, and yet, when all of its components are considered as a whole, the effect produced is one of harmony, balance and quality. The sturdy massive tang provides tremendous strength to the hilt of this long-bladed weapon.

Petersen comments on the fact that this type spans an extensive time period stretching from the early tenth century to the middle part of the eleventh century. It appears in two variants, the sword under consideration being from the later and more common.[3]

[1] The present example is also illustrated and described in Jorma Leppäaho, *Späteisenzeitliche Waffen aus Finnland: Schwertinschriften und Waffenverzierungen des 9.–12. Jahrhunderts* (Helsinki, 1964), pp. 14–15, pl. 5, 2a–e. See also *From Viking to Crusader: The Scandinavians and Europe 800 to 1200* (22nd Council of Europe Exhibition) (Copenhagen, 1992), p. 283, cat. no. 214c, where the inscription has been read as **IISOMEFECIT**.
[2] Another example in the National Museum of Finland, NM 2033:1, is shown on the same pages in Leppäaho cited above and is also included herein on pp. 122–123. The example in a private collection is illustrated and described in Ewart Oakeshott, *Records of the Medieval Sword* (Woodbridge, 1991), p. 54, as example XI.1.
[3] A further discussion of type X accompanies NM 2033:1, the sword from Padasjoki, on pp. 122–123.

← Full length view of Helsinki 11840. Photograph courtesy of and copyright National Museum of Finland, negative 28155.

↑ Detail of hilt of Helsinki 11840. Photograph courtesy of the National Museum of Finland, negative 15556, previously published in Leppäaho, p. 15, pl. 5, 2a.

↓ Drawing of the iron inlaid inscriptions from within the fuller on opposite faces of the forte of the blade. Indistinct areas in the drawing indicate indistinct areas in the actual inscriptions. Drawing by Lee A. Jones.

NM 3631:1

Date: late eleventh to early twelfth century
Find-place: Marikkovaara, Rovaniemi, Lappland, Finland
Overall length: 97.5 cm   *Blade length:* 81.7 cm
Length of cross: 14.2 cm   *Length of grip:* 9.5 cm
Balance point: 11.2 cm
Condition: excavated condition but very good

This well preserved weapon was discovered just below ground surface on Marikkovaara mountain in Rovaniemi, Lappland along with a beautifully and skilfully pattern-welded spearhead, a smaller double-barbed spearhead and a typical working axehead. It is thought probable that these artifacts were left by a traveller to Lappland who lost his way in the wilderness, some time in the twelfth century.[1]

The blade is of slender proportions, perhaps due to much use and therefore the consequence of regular honing. It terminates in an acute point with a narrow fuller running down both sides of the blade and to within a centimetre or two of the business end. The fullers and cutting edges remain extremely well defined and little corrosion has taken place. On one side of the blade is a beautifully executed iron inlaid inscription **INNOMINEDOMINII** all set within the width of the fuller, the lettering being 0.8 cm high. On the opposite side of the blade is the not so clearly discernible inscription **+GICELIN MEFE** followed by part of a **C** and a **T** and terminating with a cross. To date seven swords with identical inscriptions have been identified, six with the lettering inlaid in iron and the seventh neatly executed in silver.[2] The most outstanding of these is the splendid weapon discovered by Mr. Mark Dineley, while browsing in a second-hand bookshop in Shaftesbury.[3] The sword under examination has a massively robust tang for such a narrow blade and this feature almost certainly adds to the excellent wieldability. Unusually, the delicately sculptured cross has a gentle curve towards the blade.

Yet another remarkable feature of this sword is that it possesses a wheel pommel. This is not an isolated case as Leena Tomanterä records 15 other swords, 13 complete weapons, 2 just the pommels, but all having wheel pommels.[4] Of these a total of 8 were found at Halikko Rikala. Generally we associate the popularity of this pommel type with the mid 13th century.

The pattern-welded spearhead which accompanied this weapon is illustrated on p. 151 and is also described in Leppäaho.[5] The central lobe of decoration is most beautifully executed and remains in a remarkably fine state of preservation.

---

[1] See in particular, Jorma Leppäaho, *Späteisenzeitliche Waffen aus Finnland: Schwertinschriften und Waffenverzierungen des 9.–12. Jahrhunderts* (Helsinki, 1964), pp. 58–59; Leena Tomanterä, *Kaksi Köyliön miekkahautaa. Vanhankartanon C-kalmiston haudat XVI ja XVII* (Helsinki, 1978), pp. 31–32 and Ewart Oakeshott, *Records of the Medieval Sword* (Woodbridge, 1991), pp. 57–59.
[2] *The sword with the silver inscription is registration number 12690:479 and was found* at Halikko Rikala. During a conversation with Leena Tomanterä in 1994, she pointed out that 1b–1d on p. 59, pl. 27 of Leppäaho (1964) are indeed related to the silver inscription of sword 12690:479.

[3] Ewart Oakeshott, *Sword in the Age of Chivalry* (London, 1964), p. 34, also pl. 4b. See also Ian Peirce, 'The Development of the Medieval Sword, c. 850–1300', *Ideals and Practice of Medieval Knighthood: Papers from the Third Strawberry Hill Conference*, ed. C. Harper-Bill and Ruth Harvey (Woodbridge, 1988), pp. 146–147 and pl. 7. Also Oakeshott, *Records of the Medieval Sword*, p. 59.

[4] Tomanterä (1978), p. 61. In a later conversation with Leena, she told me additional finds had brought the total to 17 swords with wheel pommels.

[5] Leppäaho (1964), pp. 122–123, pl. 1a–b; collection number 3631:2.

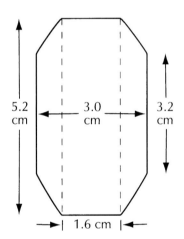

↑ Diagram of the pommel of Helsinki 3631:1 viewed in profile.

→ Helsinki 3631:1 detail of hilt. Photograph by Krister Katva courtesy of and copyright National Museum of Finland, negative 58045; previously published in Leppäaho, p. 59, pl. 27, 1a.

← Helsinki 3631:1 full length view. Photograph by H. Malmgreer (1972) courtesy of the National Museum of Finland, negative 70454.

NM 704

Date: eleventh century
Find-place: Jämsä, Finland
Overall length: 103.9 cm   *Blade length:* 88.7 cm
Length of cross: 15.1 cm   *Length of grip:* 9.3 cm
Balance point: 17 cm
Condition: excavated condition; the blade has moderate corrosion and undulating bends along its length and appears to have been caustically cleansed; towards the point there is an area of better blade preservation

This was once a most elegant weapon, which even now retains many hints of its former glory.[1]

The blade is massively long with a total length of just under 35 inches. There is evidence that this sword was used in battle, as both cutting edges of the blade have several large 'nicks' upon them. A narrow fuller of approximately 1 cm width runs down both sides of the blade to within some 19 cm of the point and extends a short distance into the tang. Most of the letters of the inscription, once picked-out in a precious metal, possibly silver, are still clearly discernible and the harsh cleansing process appears to have been responsible for the removal of any remaining inlay. The inscription reads:

The style of the lettering is very similar to that on a sword in the Nationalmuseet, Copenhagen, though the actual content of the inscriptions are different:[2]

The pommel is not completely circular, a characteristic which is totally in keeping with this type, Oakeshott A. Where the tang fits into the pommel there is a hollow recess which still retains some brown organic material.

Another sword with an inscription which exhibits the same 'handwriting' as these two is preserved in the Victoria and Albert Museum in London.[3] It was found in Whittlesea Mere, near Peterborough, in England. Ever since the time of its acquisition by the museum it has been dated to the early fourteenth century. With the more recently found and identified evidence of the sword described here, this also must be of the eleventh, not the fourteenth century.

← Helsinki NM 704 full length view. Photograph courtesy of and copyright National Museum of Finland, negative 18015.

→ Helsinki NM 704 detail of hilt. Photograph by J. Salo (1959) courtesy of and copyright National Museum of Finland, negative 23006, previously published in Leppäaho, p. 57, pl. 26 2a.

↙ Details of the inscription of Helsinki NM 704 (from Leppäaho, pp. 56–57, pl. 26 2b & 2c).

↙ Inscription on similar sword found in Denmark and presently in the Nationalmuseet in Copenhagen (from Oakeshott, *Records* XI.3, p. 55 and Oakeshott *Sword in the Age of Chivalry*, p. 35, plate 4c and p. 142, fig. 131).

[1] See Jorma Leppäaho, *Späteisenzeitliche Waffen aus Finnland: Schwertinschriften und Waffenverzierungen des 9.–12. Jahrhunderts* (Helsinki, 1964), p. 56, pl. 26, 2a–d.
[2] Ewart Oakeshott, *Sword in the Age of Chivalry* (London, 1964), p. 35 and pl. 4c. Also Ewart Oakeshott, *Records of the Medieval Sword* (Woodbridge, 1991), p. 55.
[3] Oakeshott, *Records*, p. 39, no. Xa.4 and Oakeshott, *Sword in Age of Chivalry*, pl. 48 c. and fig. 131.

NM 1174:1

Date: eleventh century, favour first half
Find-place: Leikkimäki, Kokemäki, Satakunta, Finland
Overall length: 105.2 cm   *Blade length:* 90.4 cm
Length of cross: 9.0 cm   *Length of grip:* 8.9 cm
Balance point: 28.4 cm
Condition: hilt complete and in excellent condition, though detached from the blade which is fairly good except for heavy corrosion especially towards the hilt

This splendid huge-bladed weapon belongs to a group of magnificent swords, very similar to Viking Age Scandinavian examples, mostly found in the east of the Baltic. Seventeen whole or incomplete swords of this type are known from Finland, some of them found with silver decorated spearheads, in eleventh century graves.[1] This weapon was discovered in a cemetery before 1870.

So far forward is the balance point of this sword that it is extremely doubtful that it was ever used in combat. A role as some kind of ceremonial weapon is suggested by the fact that it is beautifully decorated on all elements of the hilt. The tang does not appear to be original and it seems likely to be a poorly executed modern addition.

The silver-plated hilt is decorated with Urnes-style animals, with spirals and parmettes, and a considerable amount of the decoration has survived the rigours of time.[2] The central element of the trilobated pommel is separated from the outer portions by strips of twisted silver wire, a feature which is common among several of the other swords of this type.[3]

Even now the decoration upon the hilt is strikingly beautiful, yet it is the gold inlay upon both sides of the blade which announces the considerable importance of this weapon, both as a work of art and as an object of war or ceremony. On one side and some 20 cm from the point is a most beautifully executed 'hand of God', not in the attitude of blessing. At least four other swords bear this type of 'open hand'.[4] Further towards the hilt is a dove-like creature, perhaps the dove of peace, followed by an as yet unidentifiable inlay, then another dove followed by a another piece of inlay which defies interpretation and finally the remnants of a dove. On the reverse side and situated some 20 cm from the point, is the outline of a bishop's crozier which, when considered alongside the hand of God and the doves, may well point to the involvement of this weapon in religious ceremony. The symbols on this blade, by context of find-place and decoration of the hilt, would be most probably dated in the first half of the eleventh century, though a range from the late tenth century through to the close of the eleventh century remains possible. The inlaid inscriptions closely parallel, both in style and content, two other swords in the Schweizerischen Landesmuseum in Zurich.[5] These Swiss examples, since their finding, one in the Neuenberg lake late in the nineteenth century and the other at Yverdon, have traditionally been dated to the late thirteenth century. In the expanded context including this example from Finland, it is necessary now to re-date these swords to the eleventh century. They were both published in a doctoral dissertation in 1902 by Rudolf Wegeli, and again published in 1903 in *Zeitschrift für Waffen und Kostumkunde*, vol. 3, figs. 12 and 13. More recently they have been illustrated in Schneider's *Waffen im Schweizerischen Landesmuseum* (1980) as no. 16 and 17, pp. 22–23, and in Oakeshott's *Records of the Medieval Sword* (1991) as nos. Xa.14 and Xa.15, pp. 49–50.

[1] Several are illustrated in Jorma Leppäaho, *Späteisenzeitliche Waffen aus Finnland: Schwertinschriften und Waffenverzierungen des 9.–12. Jahrhunderts* (Helsinki, 1964), namely NM 10833:1, NM 9562:1, NM 10842:39, 34, NM 8723:194, NM 3090:10, NM 13204:393 and NM 8697,

← Helsinki 1174:1 full length view. Photograph by Jorma Leppäaho courtesy of and copyright National Museum of Finland, negative 27989.

→ Helsinki 1174:1 detail of hilt. Photograph by Jorma Leppäaho courtesy of and copyright National Museum of Finland, negative 23504.

⇶ Helsinki 1174:1 drawings of blade inscriptions. Photograph courtesy of and copyright National Museum of Finland, negative 19903, previously published in Leppäaho, p. 77, pl. 36 b & c.

pls. 33–35. See also *From Viking to Crusader: The Scandinavians and Europe 800 to 1200* (22nd Council of Europe Exhibition) (Copenhagen, 1992), cat. no. 228 and Leena Tomanterä, *Kaksi Köyliön miekkahautaa. Vanhankartanon C-kalmiston haudat XVI ja XVII* (Helsinki, 1978), pp. 62–77.
[2] According to Lena Tomanterä, the silver decoration is characteristic of Gotland and is not of a sort which she would expect to have held-up long under hard wear.
[3] See, in particular, Leppäaho, pls. 33, 34.
[4] All four had segmented polygonal pommels, per a conversation with Leena Tomanterä in 1994.
[5] Museum numbers 10116 and 7002.

National Museum of Ireland, Dublin
1988:226

Date: mid to late eleventh century
Find-place: Lough Derg (New Curraghmore), County Tipperary, Ireland
Overall length: 78.5 cm *Blade length:* 64.5 cm (found in five pieces and fitted together)
Length of cross: 11.3 cm *Length of grip:* 8.4 cm
Condition: Hilt excellent, blade in pieces but sufficiently preserved to accurately determine blade type

One of the criteria governing the swords included in this book was that they be complete, intact, specimens. I make no apologies for the inclusion of this example, much due to the unusual style of the hilt and its outstanding condition. Even now with each broken piece of blade abutted and aligned, it takes little imagination to form a picture of this weapon as it appeared somewhere between c. 1050–1100. We must be sincerely thankful that such a skilled operator as Mr. Paul Mullarky was assigned to conserve this weapon.[1]

The finely tapered blade with a deep and narrow fuller (1.0 cm width) immediately reminded me of the blade upon the sword found by Mr. Mark Dinely which has a **GICELIN MEFECIT** iron inlaid inscription upon one side and **INNOMINI DOMINI** upon the other.[2]

The blade still has large traces of wood and scabbard lining (probably leather and wool) attached to it.

The best description of this very special example is that of Raghnall Ó Floinn who states 'The pommel and guard are plain and slightly curved, and the grip is provided with a pair of mounts with scalloped inner edges.[3] These are inlaid with a border of twisted copper and silver wires and an interlaced pattern of silver wires against a niello ground. The interlaced strands terminate in plant scrolls, some of which may be debased animal heads. In form, the sword betrays Anglo-Scandinavian influences with its curved pommel and guard and scalloped mounts. The decoration is, however, purely Irish.'[4]

This inlaid decoration is paralleled on ecclesiastical metal work of the same period, namely the Clonmacnoise crozier and the bell shrine from Glankeen County, Tipperary, both places not far from where this sword was found. The hilt itself is extremely light, leading one to believe that both cross and pommel are hollow.

[1] My thanks are due to Mr. Paul Mallarky for his friendship, and the kind considerations I tend to associate with The National Museum of Ireland in Dublin and for making me aware of the splendid artifacts in the finest of museums in Europe.
[2] I have handled and studied this weapon for several hours on two separate occasions. See Ian Peirce, 'Development of the Medieval Sword c. 850–1300', *Ideals and Practice of Medieval Knighthood: Papers from the Third Strawberry Hill Conference* (1988), pp. 139–158 and Ewart Oakeshott, *The Sword in the Age of Chivalry* (London, 1964), plate 4B.
[3] See *From Viking to Crusader: The Scandinavians and Europe 800 to 1200* (22nd Council of Europe Exhibition) (Copenhagen, 1992), pp. 340–341 and cat. no. 431. This informative entry was written by Raghnall Ó Floinn of the National Museum of Ireland. Often scabbards were lined with sheep skin, wool side in whereby the lanolin protected the blade.
[4] The pommel and cross are made of copper alloy.

→ Hilted fragment of 1988:226. Photograph courtesy of and copyright by the National Museum of Ireland.

Musée de l'Armée, Paris
J4

Date: late eleventh to early twelfth century
Collection: Musée de l'Armée, Paris, accession: J4
Overall length: 85 cm *Blade length:* 72 cm
Length of cross: 19.9 cm *Length of grip:* 8 cm
Condition: hilt excellent; the blade has been much corroded and either electrolytically cleaned or treated with a caustic solution or both

The scant museum details on this important weapon state 'coming from the Pierefond's collection, 2nd Empire, Napoleon 3rd'. It is exhibited with other swords, but it is to this weapon that one's eyes are drawn. A few who will read this description are acquainted with 'The Household God' and will know precisely what I mean by the last statement. The dating of this weapon is difficult to ascertain, but I have a very powerful feeling that it is earlier rather than later.[1]

The blade of this unique sword is massively wide, with equally wide fullers extending down to within a few centimetres of the point. The cutting edges still have remarkably good definition and bear evidence of much use. The blade may well have been in a fairly good condition after excavation, but it and the hilt have a greyish tinge about them probably the result of a harsh caustic cleaning process.[2] The latter process almost certainly caused the pattern of holes which occur towards the point.

The cross is of the typical Viking *gaddhjalt* type, but in this case unusually curving gently towards the blade and tapering beautifully towards its ends. The grip is extremely broad and no doubt hides a sturdy tang.[3] The grip is covered by a neat binding of heavy gauge wire which is almost certainly tarnished silver, overlying a former probably composed of wood. Both ends of the grip are finished off with bands of silver, decorated with tram lines, into which are placed little bead-like dents in relief; a simple pattern, but hugely effective.[4] The disc pommel is very wide, to match the breadth of the blade and a little more than half an inch thick.

It is always reassuring to be able to resort to medieval manuscript illustrations for additional information, especially as manuscripts can be accurately dated by information contained in the text or by art historians and others applying their expertise to the decoration or illustrations therein. Massively broad bladed swords are rare in the eleventh and twelfth centuries, but become common during the first half of the thirteenth century and many can be seen beautifully depicted in the magnificent Maciejowski Bible, c. 1250.[5] However, the very best, and perhaps earliest, illustration of a sword closely resembling J4 may be seen in the Spanish *Beatus Commentaries on the Apocalypse* in the Archaeological Museum of Madrid, dated to the early twelfth century.[6] This illustration is hugely important, for not only does it show the earliest depiction of a faceguard attached to a helmet, but also the fully mailed warrior is holding an extremely wide bladed sword with a disc pommel. In the illustration, the pommel of the sword is in gold and there are traces of gold on the cross.[7] Another warrior in the same scene has a sword with the cross curved towards the blade like J4 which also has a gold pommel and traces of gold on the cross.[8] Jan Petersen recorded a much corroded sword from Eidnes which has a three inch (7.6 cm) blade-width at the hilt and several others with blade-widths in excess of 2.6 inches (6 cm).[9] Indeed, any sword with a blade-width in excess of 2.2 inches (5.5 cm) may be considered very rare.

[1] See Ewart Oakeshott, *The Sword in the Age of Chivalry* (London, 1964), p. 30, pl. 2b.

[2] The blade of this sword is extremely thin, as indeed it was in its youth. It needed to be, in order to produce any degree of wieldability.

[3] With such a broad blade this would be necessary.

[4] For further discussions on the grip of this sword, see Ewart Oakeshott, 'The Grip of the Medieval Sword and a Battle near Tagliacozzo', *Park Lane Arms Fair Catalogue* 11 (1994), pp. 6–7.

[5] Pierpont Morgan Library, New York, M. 638, f. 10, in particular.

[6] This important manuscript was closely examined by Mrs. Gillian Murton and myself in December, 1995 in Madrid (MS2, f. 106).

[7] See Ian Peirce, 'The Knight, His Arms and Armour c. 1150–1250', *Anglo-Norman Studies: XV. Proceedings of the Battle Conference 1992* (Woodbridge, 1993), pp. 251–274, pl. 6.

[8] It is extremely rare in medieval art for the cross of a sword to be shown gilded.

[9] See Jan Petersen, *De Norske Vikingesverd* (Oslo, 1919), p. 161, fig. 127 and p. 159, fig. 125. The sword from Snoen also has a blade-width of 3 inches; see p. 147, fig. 117.

→ Illustration from the Spanish *Beatus Commentaries on the Apocalypse* in the Archaeological Museum of Madrid, dated to the early twelfth century. Photograph courtesy of and copyright Archivo Fotográfico. Museo Arqueológico Nacional, Madrid.

← Paris J4 Overall view showing the broad, but relatively short blade. Photograph courtesy of and copyright Musée de l'Armée, Paris; negative K23718. A detailed photograph of the hilt is reproduced overleaf.

↑ Paris J4 detail of hilt with its disc pommel and long, curved and gently tapering crossguard. Photograph courtesy of and copyright Musée de l'Armée, Paris; negative K 23719.

Blade Construction and Pattern-Welding

Lee A. Jones

Rather than having been formed from a single piece of homogeneous material, the sword blades of the Viking Age, like their Migration Period and Celtic predecessors, usually have been formed by the forging together of a number of rod and or strip elements running the length of the blade. Termed a 'piled' structure, this manner of construction allowed the swordsmith to localize desired properties by joining together irons with differing properties resulting, in turn, from differing concentrations of trace elements. Requiring hardness, the cutting edges were best made of steel, which is an alloy of iron with small amounts of carbon. However, an increasing carbon content also causes increasing brittleness and too much carbon and or other trace elements, such as phosphorus, followed by the wrong heat treatment would result in a significant risk for an all-hardened steel blade to break with use. Intuitively, a bending failure offers a better chance of survival for a sword's wielder than the breaking of the blade. Between the significant and unpredictable variations in successive blooms of source metal and the limitations of a very imperfect superstitious empirical understanding of heat treatment of steel, there was a need to build a 'fail-safe' into the construction of a sword to favor bending over breaking. For this reason, softer and more malleable wrought iron or mild steel would be used for the remainder of the blade away from the tip and edges in order to impart resistance to fracture. Piled construction allowed such localization of properties to provide a sword with a hard and sharp edge with a tough backing. Another advantage, considering the variable quality of the source material, is that piled construction will tend to average the strengths and weaknesses of the individual components, much in the way that the layers of modern plywood reinforce one another. Additionally, the small rods could be carburized to increase hardness by increasing carbon content.

The technique of pattern-welding likely arose as a consequence of the piled structure of Celtic swords. If one or more of the rods or strips forming such a blade is twisted, recognizable patterns emerge which are easily manipulated. Occasional twisted strips are seen in swords dating from the late La Tène period and true pattern-welding becomes evident from about the 3rd century, reaching its zenith in terms of complexity in the 6th and 7th centuries. Late pattern-welded blades may have a thin veneer of pattern-welding over a more homogeneous iron core, suggesting that, while pattern-welding may have evolved as a consequence of a piled structure, in the end it was a decorative process. Pattern-welding is generally considered to have passed out of use by the close of the Viking Age, though it has since recurred in the edged weapons of many other cultures.

Cross-Sections Showing Variations in Construction of Viking Age Double-Edged Sword Blades

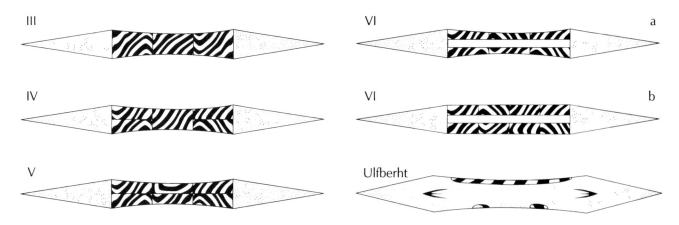

↑ The diagrams designated by Roman numerals have been labelled after the scheme presented in fig. 103 on p. 246 of R.F. Tylecote and B.J.J. Gilmour, *B.A.R. British Series 155: The Metallography of Early Ferrous Edge Tools and Edged Weapons* (Oxford, 1986). Just about any cross-sectional possibility which could be inferred from surface examination of excavated pattern-welded swords has been confirmed by metallographic studies. Type III represents a blade having, in this example, three pattern-welded rods welded one to another side by side and forming a core to which have been attached steel edges. Metallographic studies frequently show the edge sections to also be of complex composite structure. The core of type IV incorporates a central rod, which is exposed on either surface of the blade, to which have been attached two rods on either side, each of these additional four rods being exposed on one blade face only. Type V employs an even number of rods welded back to back, with half visible on each blade face. In type VI, half of the rods are visible on each blade face, but a central core has been added. Types V and VI are the forms most commonly encountered. The illustration labelled VI b represents one of the early Geibig type 1 blades which lack fullers. Also shown is an **ULFBERHT** style blade, after Alan R. Williams, 'Methods of Manufacture of Swords in Medieval Europe: Illustrated by the Metallography of Some Examples', *Gladius* 13 (1977), pp. 75–101. These blades were built up from a complex piled structure, with steel in the edges and the lowest carbon concentrations at the core. Vestigial pattern welding is present in the form of a thin inlay forming the smith's name or geometric patterns, see also the illustration on p. 8.

↓ Detail of patterns evident on the surface of a double-edged sword found in a third to fourth century votive bog deposit at Nydam, C25340 in the Nationalmuseet, Copenhagen. This is not classical pattern-welding, but rather a lattice made up of iron inlays overlain one on top of another. While such inlays are often thought of as a late feature, this Roman Iron Age blade, as well as the Migration Age blade shown on pp. 148–149 are both evidence of early application of such technique. A large number of pattern-welded blades were also recovered from the Nydam site. Photograph courtesy of and copyright the National Museum of Denmark, negative I555.

→ Both the straight (*streifendamast*) and curved (*rosendamast*) patterns which are observed in a pattern-welded blade ultimately arise from the same process of twisting a laminated rod made up of alternating layers of contrasting materials. The pattern which develops is a function of the depth to which the rod is ultimately exposed by grinding and polishing, the extent to which the rod had been twisted and the number of layers in the starting laminated rod.

In the diagram at right, a clay model of a rod composed of sixteen alternating layers prepared by bladesmith Dan Maragni was twisted and then progressively ground, forming a facet along its length which was photographed at regular intervals. The percentage of reduction in the overall thickness of the rod is shown in the scale, such that 50% represents the centre of the rod. Were the rod further levelled, a mirror image of the patterns first disclosed would be exposed.

Depending upon the ultimate design desired, the rods may be twisted at varying intervals, either to the left or right, or allowed to remain straight. After preparation of the component rods, the next stage is their assembly into a blade, where rods with complementary twist patterns are ultimately installed side-by-side to form a central pattern-welded panel.

The rods actually used in making these swords are frequently found to contain seven alternating layers of varyingly dissimilar irons. Variations in carbon content are associated with subtle differences in surface colour following etching, though patterns will also emerge to some degree even when similar iron is used in all layers owing to slag inclusions and trace elements added by the flux used in welding. Increased contrast between the layers could be achieved by use of phosphorus rich iron, which remains lighter in colour when etched by mildly acidic agents.

Janet Lang and Barry Ager, 'Swords of the Anglo-Saxon and Viking Periods in the British Museum: a Radiographic Study', *Weapons and Warfare in Anglo-Saxon England*, ed. Sonia Chadwick Hawkes (Oxford, 1989), pp. 85–122.

Herbert Maryon, 'Pattern-welding and Damascening of Sword-blades: Part I–Pattern-Welding', *Studies in Conservation* 5 (1960), pp. 25–37.

Lena Thålin-Bergman, 'Blacksmithing in Prehistoric Sweden', *Iron and Man in Prehistoric Sweden,* ed. Karin Calissendorff, et al. (Stockholm, 1979), pp. 99–133.

Development of Patterns from a Laminated Twisted Rod

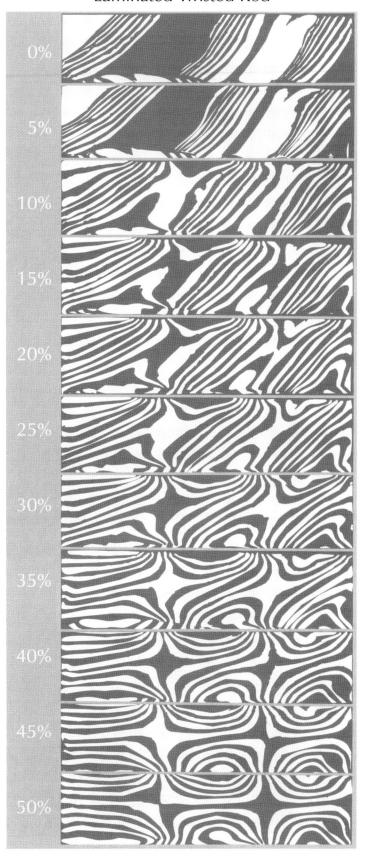

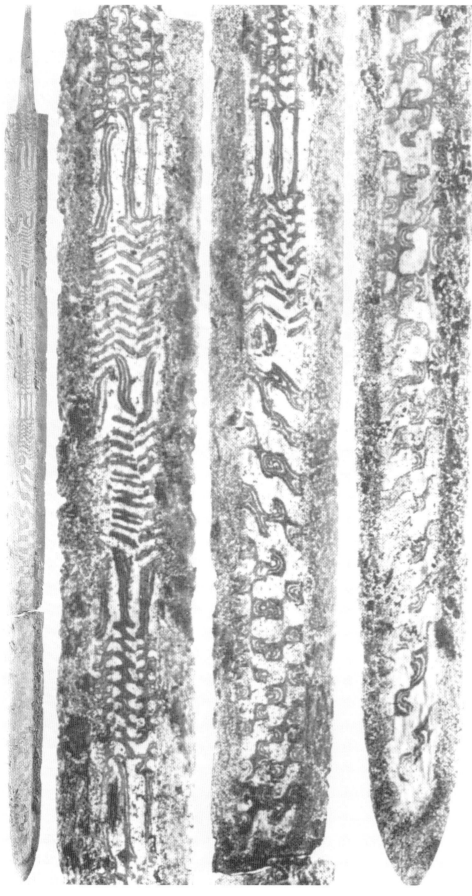

← NM 2022:1 from Vehmaa, Lahdinko, Huolila, dated to the 8th century. The side shown above has three bands of pattern-welding visible in the forte of the blade, near the hilt, each about 0.7 cm in width. Areas forming a straight repeating diagonal characteristic of a peripheral section of a twisted rod may be seen and alternate with straight areas. When oppositely twisted rods are welded side by side and ground to this shallow depth, a herringbone or chevron pattern such as this is formed. Further down the blade a curved pattern characteristic of about 25% of the rod having been ground away is seen, beyond which the pattern rapidly transforms into two bands, each 1 cm in width, which form a checquer-board pattern characteristic of the center of a twisted rod.

Photograph by Jorma Leppäaho courtesy of and copyright National Museum of Finland, previously published in Jorma Leppäaho, *Späteisenzeitliche Waffen aus Finnland: Schwertinschriften und Waffenverzierungen des 9.– 12. Jahrhunderts* (Helsinki, 1964) pp. 66–67, pl. 31.

→ The pattern on the opposite surface of the blade begins as two bands of curved pattern, each 1.3 cm wide. A zone of corrosion obscures the pattern in a zone several centimetres from the tang, just beyond which are two inlaid iron strips perpendicular to the length of the blade which cover the fuller. Beyond this, three bands of diagonal pattern alternate with straight areas until the mid-portion of the blade, where the central band lifts above its adjacent companions and transforms into a wavy serpent-like inlay alternatingly covering the remaining two bands and what appears to be an untwisted rod in between as it makes its undulations approaching the tip. The changes in numbers of bands upon a blade face and the transformation of a band into an overlay are both unusual features.

Photograph by Jorma Leppäaho courtesy of and copyright National Museum of Finland, previously published in Jorma Leppäaho, *Späteisenzeitliche Waffen aus Finnland: Schwertinschriften und Waffenverzierungen des 9.–12. Jahrhunderts* (Helsinki, 1964) pp. 68–69, pl. 32.

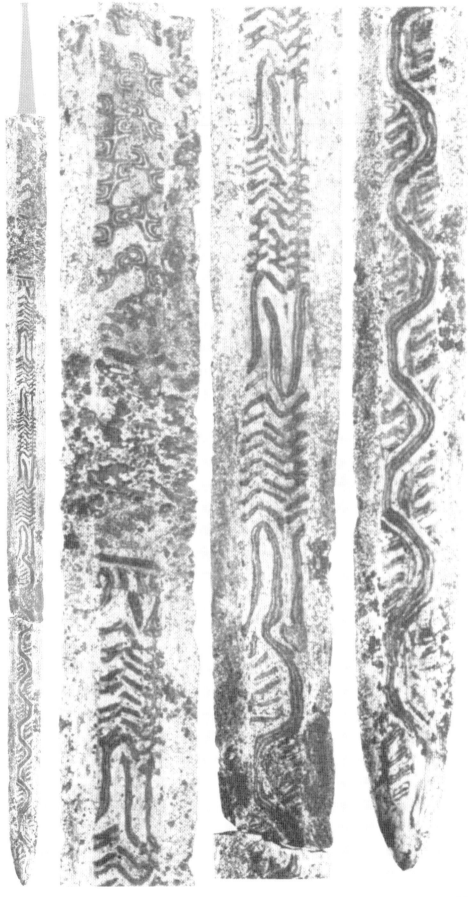

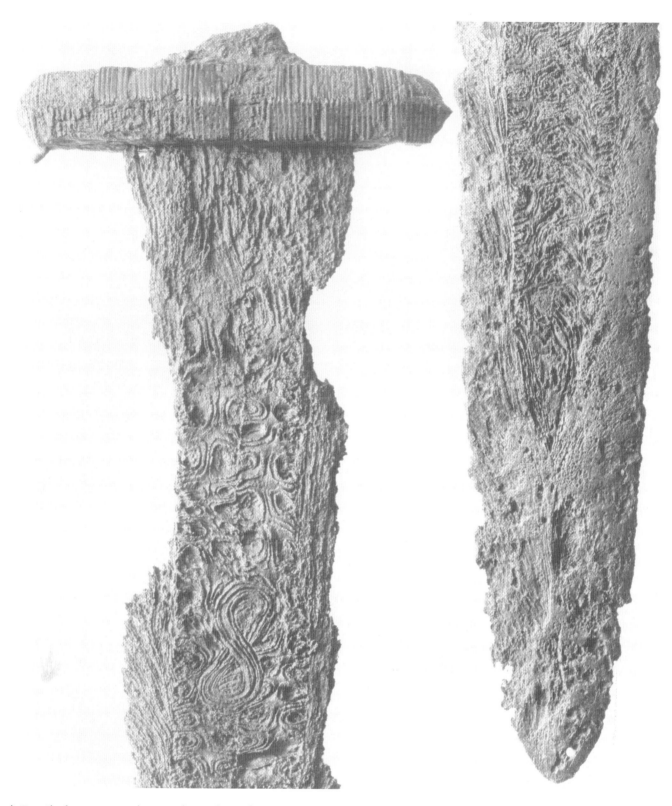

↑ Detail of patterns evident on the surface of C6374 in the Nationalmuseet, Copenhagen. The photograph to the left, which includes the crossguard, shows a blade with two bands of pattern-welding having semicircular reflecting curves indicating that the plane of section through the twisted rods is very near to the centre. An iron inlay in the from of an '8', as viewed, is also present. In the photograph on the right, the same pattern continues into the tip. The manner in which the pattern-welded panel tapers and terminates within the tip is typical. Photographs courtesy of and copyright the National Museum of Denmark, negative 13315 (left) and 13316 (right).

→ Full length view and detail of a pattern-welded spear, Helsinki 3631:2, found on Marikkovaara mountain in Rovaniemi, Lappland together with the sword illustrated and described on pp. 134–135. The style of the spear is consistent with the eleventh to twelfth century dating given for the sword. Photographs by E. Laakso courtesy of and copyright National Museum of Finland, negatives 14823 and 21281, respectively; previously published in Leppäaho, p. 123, pl. 59, 1a & 1b.

Just as with swords, the spear blades of these times have a piled structure, that is, they are built up of multiple components, ideally having good quality steel at the edge, tough iron at the core and, in a decorated example such as this, contrasting alloys to form the pattern. Tylecote and Gilmour, cited below, carried out metallographic studies of another spear with similar surface patterns found in the Thames near the ford at Kempsford in Gloucestershire. A section from one half of that spear disclosed ten discrete components, implying that the full cross-section would include double that, or twenty. In that specimen, a narrow hardened steel edge was supported between two considerably wider iron plates, occupying the position of the lighter metal next to both edges in the photograph on the right. The serrated or regularly wavy boundary between this and the darkly staining adjacent metal marks a full thickness weld boundary. Tylecote and Gilmour concluded that the components forming this join would have been corrugated such that they would interlock before they were welded together. This dark layer is welded to another layer of lightly staining alloy, which in turn is welded to an iron core which supports two thin strips of typical pattern-welding, one visible on each face.

A. Anteins, 'Die Kurischen Rhombischen Lanzenspitzen mit Damasziertem Blatt', *Gladius* VII (1968), pp. 5–26.

R.F. Tylecote and B.J.J. Gilmour, *B.A.R. British Series 155: The Metallography of Early Ferrous Edge Tools and Edged Weapons* (Oxford, 1986), pp. 119–123.

Jaap Ypey 'Flügellanzen in niederländischen Sammlungen', *Vor- und Frühgeschichte des unteren Niederrheins. Quellenschriften zur westdeutschen Vor- und Frühgeschichte* 10 (1982), pp. 241–267.

Index

Blade
bent, 87–88
chronology, 21–24
classification, 15
classification, Geibig, 20–24, *diagram*, 22
classification, Oakeshott
type X, 124–125, 128, 130, 142
type Xa, 24, 131–133
type XI, 24, 134–137
type XII, 138–139
construction, 26, 28,30, 145–151
decoration
crozier, 138–139
dove, 138–139
religious, 138
hand of God, 138–139
dimensions, 21–24
balance point, 7, 21, 22
taper, 21–24, 40, 100, 124, 126
thickness, 21, 23–24, 76
width, 32, 38, 64, 74–75, 77, 82, 84, 96, 142–143
edge, honing, 84, 106
edge, nicks, 80, 97, 120
elements, trace, 26
form, evolution of, 6–7
inlay,
brass, 10
gold, 10, 129, 138–139
iron, 34–35, 46, 74–75, 77–78, 80–82, 90, 96, 115, 120, 122–125, 131–134, 146, 148–150
geometric, 23, 95–96, 98, 100–101, III
serpentine, 52, 148–149
symbols, 110
silver, 10, 109, 128–129
soft metal, 136–137
inscriptions, 6, 10, 110
Atalbald, 8
Banto, 8
Benno, 8
Cerolt, 54
Duna, 120
Gecelin me fecit, 8, 134
Ibnatis, 90
In Nomine Domini & variants, 9, 24, 132–134
Ingelrii, 8, 23, 60–61, 80–81, 90, 122
Inlerurieiti, 122–123
Inno me fecit, 8
Leutfrit, 8
Leutlrit, 77–78
Niso me fecit & variants, 8, 132–133
religious, 9
Shvaimivahs, 109
Sinimi~ini~is, 109
Sitanbi, 90

Sivineviwinis, 109
Ulfberht & variants, 7–9, 23, 54–55, 63–64, 95–96, 98, 100–101,124–125, III
length of, 96
manufacturing origin, 7
profile, 52, 54
repair, welded, 38, 52, 118
short, 90, 95
shortened, 100
single-edged, 20–21, 39–40, 47–50
Blodiða, 40, 118
Carbon, influencing colour, 147
Classification, difficulties, 15–16
Crossguard
curved, 74–75, 77–79, 82–83, 109, 116–117
hollow, 109
thickness, 89
Einvigi, type of duel, 11
Find-places, 3
bog, 50, 63
grave, 6, 13, 32, 38–40, 42, 58, 68, 72, 84, 86–87, 92, 94, 102, 116
ground, 36, 112
lake, 44, 95, 106, VI
marsh, 82
river, 13, 28, 34, 48, 54, 56, 74, 77, 80, 84, 90, 98, 100, 104, 110, 131
stream, 76
tomb, 104
Flux, effect on patterns, 147
Fuller
absence, 21
dimensions
depth, 127
taper, 22–24
width, 20–24, 72, 77
Gaddhjalt, 5, 122, 131, 142, 144
Glødeskall, 36, 38, 40, 68, 87, 94, 116, 127
Goethite, 77, 80
Grip
ferrule, 42–43, 74–75, 95
leather covered, VII
metal, 44
wire covered, 104–105, 142
wood, 34–35, 74–75
Guards
absence of upper, 16
curved, 16, 19–20, 92–93
ridged, 46
scrolled, 47
Hilt, 15–16
Abington, 76
classification, 15–20
classification, Behmer
type V, 46
type VI, 30
type VIII, 28, 46

classification, Geibig, 16
classification, Jakobsson, 16
classification, Oakeshott
type VIII, 5
type IX, 5
classification, Petersen, 15–20; *diagram*, 18–19
distinctive type 1, 17–18, 30–33, IV
distinctive type 2, 17–18, 46
type A, 16–18, 28–29
type B, 16–18, 21, 34–35
type C, 17–18, 21, 36–41
type D, 17–18, 42–45
type E, 17–18, 46, 49
type F, 18, 21, 47
type G, 18–21, 47
type H, 17–18, 21, 34, 48–62, V–VI
type I, 17–18, VII
type K, 19–20, 63–73
type L, 19–20, 74–83
type M, 19–21, 84–86
type N, 18, 86
type O, 19–20, 87–91, VI
type P, 19, 92–93
type Q, 20, 94–95
type R, 19–20, 96–97
type S, 19–20, 98–107
type T, 19–20, 108–109, VIII
type U, 18, 20, 110–113
type V, 18, 20, 114
type W, 18, 114
type X, 18, 20, 115–125
type Y, 19, 126
type Z, 19, 127
type Æ, 19–20
classification, Wheeler, 3–5, 15–16; *diagram*, 3
type I, 3–4, 84–86
type II, 3–4, 36–41, 48–62
type III, 4, 96–107
type IV, 4, 6, 63–73
type V, 4, 6, 74–76
type VI, 4, 20, 77–81
type VII, 4–5, 20, 110–113
construction, 30–31
copper alloy, 140
decoration, 5–6
absence of, 39, 47, 94–95
Anglo-Saxon, 20, 76
animal, 17, 32, 76, 128–129
array of depressions, 46
brass, 6, 17, 44, 48–50, 90, V–VI
bronze, 6, 46, 56–57, 68, 88–89, 114, IV
copper, 17, 32, 34–35, 42–43, 54–55, 60–62,

77–79, 92–93, 96–98, 102–105, 110, 140, IV, VII
geometric, 76
gold, 6, 30, 42–43
gripping beast ornament, 30–31, IV
interlace, 96–97, 102–108, 140
Irish ecclesiastical, 140
Jelling style, 106
knot motif, 89, VI
letters, 128–129
Maltese cross, 127
Mammen style, 98, 104–107
manner of application, 127
niello, 6, 20
plant, 76
plated, 64, 66–67
silver, 6, 17, 28, 30–32, 42–44, 46, 54–67, 70–71, 74–80, 92–93, 96, 98, 100–108, 110, 112–113, 114, 127, 138–140, IV, VI–VIII
tin, 6
Trewhiddle style, 20, 76
twisted wire, 42–43
Urnes style, 138
vine scroll, 63–67
wire, 44, 50, 52–59, 66–67, 70–71, 74–75, 92–93, 112–113, 138–140, V–VII
evolution of, 6, 46
inscriptions upon
Hartoifa, 66
Hartolfr, 66
Hiltipreht, 4, 63
Mannheim type, 17–18
rivet heads, false, 6, 16, 30, 31
rivets, 17, 51, 58, 68, 77, 90, 100
absence of rivets, 88
spikehilt, 5, 122, 131, 142, 144
upper, single piece, 114
Holmgang, type of duel, 11
Iron, best sources, 3
Kenning, 1–2
Manuscripts, as means of dating, 142
Pattern-welding, 7, 21, 26–27, 30–32, 34–35, 40–41, 44, 56, 68–69, 74, 76, 88, 104, 112, 115, 118, 145–151, I–II, V
Phosphorus, influencing colour, 147
Pommel
absence, 16, 20, 84, 92
Brazil nut, 5, 18, 122–123, 132–133
bronze, 114, VI
cocked hat, 5, 126
conjoined with upper

guard, 17, 118–119
dimensions, 135, VI
disc, 5, 10, 18, 128, 130, 142–144
disc, eccentric, 136–137
fixed to tang, 17, 46
hollow, 30
lobated, 17–20
five-lobed, 4, 16, 20, 64–65, 68, 72–73, 87–89, 96, 102–107, 127
seven-lobed, 16, 20, 70–71
three-lobed, 4, 16, 46, 74–75, 77–79, 100–101, 110, 112, 114, 138–139
rounding of underside, 20
semicircular, 46, 86, 114
single piece, 20, 72–73, 80–81, 110, 115–116, 118, 120, 122–123
small, 47
tea-cosy, 116, 132–133
thickness, 89
triangular, 16–17
weight, 84
wheel, 5, 10, 18, 134–135
zoomorphic, 4, 17, 46
Rosendamast, 147
Sagas
duels, 10–13
Egil's saga, 11–12
Eyrbryggja Saga, 12–13
Kormac's Saga, 11
Song of Roland, 13
Scabbard
chape, 30–31
leather lining, residual, V
nature of lining, 140
wood, residual, V
Spear, 10, 64, 134, 151
Streifendamast, 147
Sword
Baltic region, 138–139
boy's, 86, 95
Celtic, 145
Chertsey, 100
cultural importance, 1–2, 13–14
design, persistence of features, 16
destruction of, ritual, 6, 68, 87, 102, 127
dimensions, 20–24
length, 36
weight, 36, 40, 42
distribution, 16
duration of use, 2, 6, 15
Migration Period, 145–146
names, 1–2, 11–13
register of examples, vi
Tang
shim, bronze, V
width, 127
Véttrim, see grip, ferrule
Welding, scarf, 10